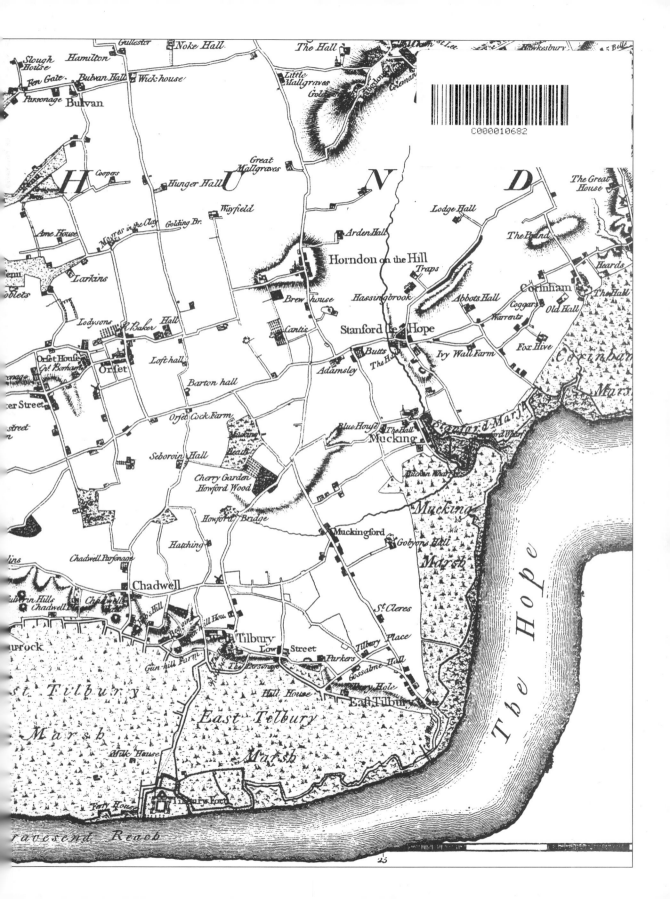

Grays Thurrock

A HISTORY

On 1 September 1914 a huge crowd of onlookers waited for the newly recruited Army Volunteers to march up High Street to board trains at the station. The continental-style circular urinal was removed to allow a war memorial to be built after the end of the war. The scene is recorded by Menlove, the Grays photographer.

Grays Thurrock

A HISTORY

Brian Evans

Phillimore

2004

Published by
PHILLIMORE & CO. LTD
Shopwyke Manor Barn, Chichester, West Sussex, England

ISBN 1 86077 305 2

Printed and bound in Great Britain by
CAMBRIDGE PRINTING

To Susan
'The Incomparable'

Map of Grays in the mid-1950s

Contents

☙

List of Illustrations		ix
Acknowledgements		xi
	Introduction	1
1	Through the Centuries	3
2	Grays: From Little Port to Growing Town	18
3	The River Thames	37
4	Villages of the Hidden East	43
5	Northward along the Heights	61
6	Westward Prospects	71
7	Industrial Revolutions	89
8	Only Connect: The Story of Transport	103
9	On the Front Line	113
10	Thurrock Since 1945	127
	Bibliography	129
	Index	131

List of Illustrations

☙

Frontispiece: Waiting for the Volunteers, Grays, 1914

1	Ancient route through Hangmans Wood, 1887	1
2	Thurrock map, 1936	2
3	Hangmans Wood path, *c.*1930	2
4&5	Palaeolithic boring tool and fossil antler	4
6	Bronze-Age axe	5
7	Romano-British pottery from Tilbury	5
8	Denehole investigation no.5, 1887	6
9	Plan of the Denehole pits, 1887	7
10	Saxon bucket from Mucking	9
11	Saxon bucket from Mucking excavation	10
12	Turold of Rochester	13
13	Henry de Gray's grant	14
14	Ralph de Knevynton brass	15
15	Sheep bells from Tilbury	16
16	Saxon glass horn	17
17	St Peter and St Paul, Grays, in 1807	19
18	Church corner, South Street, 1930s	20
19	Palmers School about 1929	22
20	Lanham and Pennington, tailors	22
21	Whitehall Road, 1910	23
22	Thurrock United F.C. in 1927	24
23	Grays F.C. at the Recreation Ground	24
24	Empire Theatre and shops, Grays High Street	25
25	A glimpse of Grays Market, 1950s	25
26	Joyes Ltd, Easter ladieswear advert	26
27	Horncastles Stores advert, 1930	27
28	Old Hall Farm, Orsett, 1930	27
29	Southend Road, Socketts Heath, 1950s	28
30	Salmon's Stores delivery van	28
31	New Road, Grays in 1905	29
32	W. Cockley's stall, Sports Day, *c.*1920	30
33	Orsett High Road, 1940s	32
34	Looking towards *Whitmore Arms*, Orsett, 1920s	32
35	Southend Road near Palmers School corner, 1912	34
36	New Road, Grays, 1912	35
37	Top of Bridge Road, 1912	35
38	Police on strike duty at Grays, 1912	36
39	Sailing craft, Purfleet, *c.*1920	37
40	East Indiaman of the 17th century	38
41	Tilbury Docks railway system	39
42	Opening of Docks	39
43	The Basin, Tilbury Docks, 1912	39
44	Orient Line Berths, aerial view of Tilbury	40
45	Central Dock, Tilbury	40
46	Tilbury Hailing Station, 1950s	40
47	Seamen's Hospital, Tilbury, *c.*1920	41
48	Norwegian Seamen's Mission	41
49	SS *Armadale*, 1925	42
50	Rectory Road, Little Thurrock	43
51	*Ship Inn*, Little Thurrock	44
52	'Sleepers' farmhouse, Chadwell St Mary	46
53	St Mary's Church and *Cross Keys*, Chadwell	46
54	'Balstonia': Homesteads Ltd advert	48
55	Aerial view of Stanford, *c.*1930	49
56	High Street, Stanford-le-Hope, 1907	50
57	The *Bull* at Corringham	52
58	Wooden houses at Corringham, *c.*1900	52
59	East Tilbury cottages	55
60	East Tilbury Rectory at the end of the 19th century	55

61   Drover, Tilbury Marsh, 1900 56
62   Tilbury Fort, c.1800. 57
63   Smuggler's signal lantern 58
64   St Michael's tower, Fobbing. 58
65   *White Lion*, Fobbing 59
66   The Chase, South Ockendon, c.1905 61
67   Moat, bridge and gateway,
     South Ockendon Hall 62
68   South Ockendon village centre, 1900. 64
69   North Road, South Ockendon
     showing shops, 1920s 65
70   Horndon-on-the-Hill, South Hill, 1930s 65
71   Country lane and St Peter and
     St Paul's, Horndon. 66
72   Near the *Swan* inn, Horndon, 1930s. 67
73   Bulphan Schoolhouse, c.1910 67
74   Edwardian Dry Street 68
75   Fen Lane, Bulphan, 1940s 70
76   Thatched cottage, North Stifford 72
77   North Stifford, 1920s 72
78   West Thurrock Schools, c.1913 74
79   Teece's shop, West Thurrock. 75
80   Botany Terrace, 1908 76
81   Purfleet beach, 1908 78
82   Avenue North Buildings, 1904. 80
83   Railway Terrace, 1913 81
84   Cox and Palmer's Tea Garden, Purfleet. 81
85   Purfleet Crossing, 1894 82
86   Training Ship *Cornwall* at Purfleet, 1894. 83
87   High Street, Aveley 84
88   High Street, Aveley, 1915 85
89   The Lodge, Aveley, 1903 85
90   Purfleet Road, Aveley, 1918 86
91   Belhus, south drawing room 87
92   Belhus Mansion in the 18th century 88
93   The great fireplace from Belhus. 88
94   Aveley Mill, May 1902. 90
95   Whitbread's chalk quarry, Purfleet 91
96   Fishing vessels near Belmont Castle 92
97   Scotch smacks in the Thames. 92
98   Purfleet Deep Water Wharf locomotive 93
99   Little Thurrock brickworks receipt. 94
100 The Dutch House, Grays. 95
101 Gas holder, London Road 96
102 Seabrooke Brewery delivery cart, 1912 97
103 Beer crate from price list. 97
104 Map of Grays industrial works, early
     20th century 98

105 Essex Board, Welfare Hall, Purfleet. 99
106 The Queen at TBM, 1953 100
107 Fiberite packs from TBM 100
108 Shoe factory building, 1930s 101
109 Bata's, East Tilbury 102
110 Ciment Fondu advert 102
111 Ferry boat *Edith* .103
112 Announcement of Grays Pier
     Company, 1842 .104
113 *World's End*, Tilbury Fort 104
114 Tilbury ferryboat *Rose* in the 1940s 105
115 Landing Stage and Station,
     Tilbury Riverside .105
116 Station Gardens, South Ockendon, c.1900. 106
117 LTSR locomotive, *Corringham* 107
118 Porter and grandchild, South Ockendon
     Station, c.1900 107
119 Stanford-le-Hope Station, early 20th century . . .108
120 Works, railways and sidings scene,
     West Thurrock, 1950s 108
121 Corringham Railway 0-6-0 locomotive
     at Corringham. 109
122 Kynochtown (later Coryton) Station 109
123 Stanford and District bus. 110
124 No.374 bus (Grays to West Thurrock) 112
125 No.370 route bus in LT livery 112
126 Harris Coach and driver 112
127 Armada Camp playing card 114
128 Tilbury Fort guarded by a 'redcoat' soldier 115
129 Coalhouse Fort gateway 115
130 Lightning strike at Ordnance Board
     House, Purfleet 116
131 Purfleet Garrison gateway 117
132 View of Purfleet, 1807. 117
133 HMS *Thunderer* passes Purfleet, 1912 118
134 Rail system, Coalhouse Fort 118
135 The Royal Engineers camp, Purfleet 119
136 Private F. Reeve of Grays with wounded
     soldiers in hospital 120
137 Graf Zeppelin passes over Grays, 1930s. 122
138 Second World War flying bomb 122
139 Badge of the 6th Anti-Aircraft division
     (Thames Estuary, etc.). 122
140 National Savings advert, *Grays and
     Thurrock Gazette* .123
141 Soldiers *en route* for Purfleet rifle range 124
142 Radar/listening tower, East Tilbury 124
143 Wartime AA site, Coalhouse Fort. 126

Acknowledgements

❦

M.U. Jones, illustration 13, Donald Maxwell family, illustration 61, Bob Drake (Atticus books) illustrations 137 and 141, and Keith Langridge, illustrations 56, 60, 96, 135-6, 145-6. All other illustrations are from the author's private collection.

Horrified onlookers watch the burning of the Training Ship *Goliath* at her moorings off Grays on 22 December 1875. Her full complement consisted of 520 boys and officers.

Introduction

Thurrock is one of the most interesting and remarkable areas in England and perhaps the most unappreciated outside the district. Although for most of the passing centuries the land and people lay in an apparent backwater untouched by national events, the locality occasionally became an important backdrop to some momentous event or the life of a significant leader. Nearly every one of Thurrock's communities has a story to tell. A strong thread binds the villages and towns together, and makes the district seem like a small county detached from the rest of Essex, with its own individual character.

The story of Thurrock's industrial development is a remarkable one, beginning with the early extractive trades and their sites, some of which provided a location for water and gas works and later industrial production when worked out. The range of products manufactured or converted along the Thames Bank in the late 19th and 20th centuries was a microcosm of those produced in the whole of Britain, and led to the south of our area assuming some of the characteristics of communities in the Midlands and north of England, such as networks of railway sidings and lines running across the highway, uniformed bands and generations of the same family working for a firm which provided for their welfare and recreation.

Behind this southern belt lay quite a few acres of farmland, and the importance of yeomen and gentlemen farmers, for instance, led to Orsett, a farming community with a lord of the manor, becoming a dominant seat of local government for a time, with the local workhouse situated at the centre of a green landscape featuring

1   The path through Hangmans Wood, 1887. This is believed to be part of a very ancient way, which led from East Tilbury, and a causeway/ferry across the Thames.

1

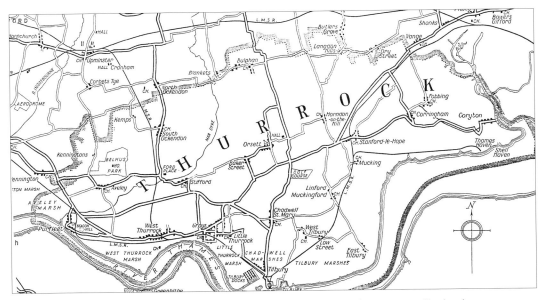

2 Thurrock Urban District as created on 1 April 1936, bringing together many smaller local government areas, such as Orsett, Tilbury, Purfleet and Grays. The nature of this consolidation was ahead of its time, creating what we would today call a regional authority.

windmills, country churches and centuries-old houses.

Thurrock's riverside area had links with the rest of the world through the mighty Thames highway via wharves and jetties. Grays High Street was once a Sailortown with many Jack Tars and bargemen frequenting its numerous inns and taverns, marine suppliers and lodging houses. Tilbury became a place of entry and departure in the earlier half of the 20th century, with a stop-over hotel for world travellers on the big ocean liners, and from that time on was also a deep-water trading port.

Many other features marking Thurrock out as a very special area of interest are highlighted in this book.

3 The Hangmans Wood path, *c.*1930. The ancient way was later known as the Coal Road and used to bring coal inland.

ONE

Through the Centuries

In 1964, during the normal working of gravel and clay at the Tunnel Portland Cement pit in Aveley, John Hesketh noticed that some fossilised bones had been unearthed. The British Museum's natural history section, called in as a result, proved that the remains were the fossilised skeletons of both a mammoth and an elephant, about 200,000 years old but in fact probably from different prehistoric periods. These animals, together with the remains of smaller creatures which roamed the landscape of Thurrock at this distant time, fed at a watering hole surrounded by peat bogs. Although they became trapped at different periods, they were preserved at the same spot. The mammoth was on the local scene during the Pleistocene era, which was a Glacial, or Ice, Age. This immense beast had a hide covered with thick hair and tusks which could be more than six feet long, curling outwards and then inwards again at the tip. The other skeleton belonged to a straight-toothed elephant, which may have stood 14 feet at the shoulder. The pair show the great climatic changes that occurred in the locality as in the rest of Britain: the mammoth lived during a cold phase, thriving in the conditions, while the elephant enjoyed a warm interglacial phase.

A later period is represented by remains found just across the river. The reconstruction of Swanscombe Man, as he is called, is evidence of a clan group or small tribe who lived by hunting deer and other small animals in a warm climate, enabling the development of the species in favourable conditions. These peoples inhabited the margins of the Thames at least 100,000 years ago.

Background work shows the gradual changes of environment over many thousands of years. The lower loams and gravels point to an era of grassy mud-flats interspersed by little streams. This landscape would be edged by hazel scrub merging into mixed oak forest. All the resources were present here for a hunting and gathering life. Animals such as elephant, rhinoceros, horse and deer could be hunted to provide food. Birds and fish could be taken from the waters and marshes. The gravel terraces behind provided a ready source of flint for the manufacture of small hunting implements and for other daily use. The use of cores and flakes rather than hand-axes is known as a 'chopper-core' industry (Clactonian type). At the Whitehall Lane pit on the eastern side of Grays are what are known as

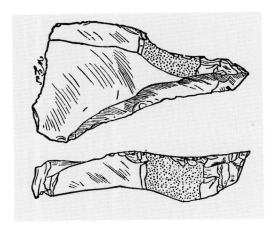

4 & 5 Evidence of Palaeolithic man in Little Thurrock: boring tool (*above*) and fossil antler with signs of shaping (at marked points) into working tool.

Ilford Terrace deposits on a bench level of 49 ft. O.D. These have yielded flint implements, indicating that this type of Clactonian flint industry was active in Thurrock. In July 1957 a large Palaeolithic hand-axe of ochraceous flint was unearthed, twelve feet down on the site of Thurrock Technical College, perhaps dating from the stage after the 'chopper-core' era.

Tilbury Man

During the excavation of Tilbury Docks in 1883 'Tilbury Man' was unearthed from 30 feet below the surface. The skeleton was carefully lifted out by Sir Richard Owen, who considered it to date from the early Stone Age; other experts compared it with the Neanderthal man whose remains, found by the Rhine in 1857, were from a later era.

T.V. Holmes thought the Tilbury specimen very similar to 'the robust but coarse featured people of the round barrows of south-west England and of the Bronze Age'. F.J.C. Spurrell believed that he could possibly have been a transition between Palaeolithic and Neolithic man, which would make him contemporary with both the mammoth and the elephant.

The world famous Mucking archaeological site was explored from the late 1960s into the 1970s, revealing evidence of occupation by successive early inhabitants, from the Stone Age to the Medieval period. Here, late Neolithic examples of Beaker Pottery emerged. A large vessel was decorated by 'whipped twisted card' round a sharp-edged flint flake, which produced a very typical toothed design. Small sherds of Beaker Pottery could be compared with other examples from Dublin, south-west Scotland, Northumberland, East Anglia and the Continent. The Beaker people are often thought of as the first farmers, and could have walked over from the Continent at a time when England was still joined to the European land mass.

Bronze Age

The transitional Neolithic stage known as the late or Beaker period saw our native population becoming aware of the value of metalworking through contacts with itinerant users and traders. This led to the dual use of stone and metal between c.1800 and 1500 BC. There occurred an age of invading warriors, who subjugated the natives, formed an aristocracy and spread the trading influence from Ireland, Brittany and northern Europe. Many would have entered Britain via the Thames. The ensuing Middle Bronze Age saw herdsmen migrating with their animals. Two examples of the bronze palstave axe

6 (*left*)   Bronze-Age socketed axe owned by an early dweller in Corringham.

7 (*below*)   Pottery from Romano-British huts at Tilbury.

from this time have been found in Grays. Round about 1000 BC a further wave of immigrants ushered in the Late Bronze Age with a wider use of the metal, hoards of broken and damaged tools and lumps of re-smelted ore and metal being discovered in recent times. A number of these were at coastal and river boundaries and it seems that itinerant metalworkers were travelling by water and leaving hoards as a form of currency, to be reclaimed at a later date. One of these caches from Grays contained 309 items and it seems that Grays may have formed a centre of occupation during Late Bronze-Age times.

Iron users appeared in Britain about 600 BC firstly as traders and raiders. About 500 BC they seem to have appeared on our shores in great numbers. Their earlier bases had been Hallstatt in Austria and near the mouth of the Rhine. In Thurrock, one of their early incursions inland from the Thames has been discovered at Linford. Excavations at what is known as an Iron Age 'A' settlement (from the earliest period) found fragmentary traces of a circular hut, two hearths and rubbish pits with pottery including a food vessel. The incomers did not completely swamp their forerunners; change was gradual. Evidence of Bronze-Age decorations on Iron-Age-type pottery has been seen at an Aveley dig, suggesting intermarriage and slowly changing lifestyles. In a field at East Tilbury during a dry summer (1959) two concentric rings of lush growth, in diameter about 100 feet and 35 feet respectively, were investigated. At the very centre of them was a cairn 22 inches in diameter and 14 inches high, the tip being 10 inches below the surface. A Bronze-Age

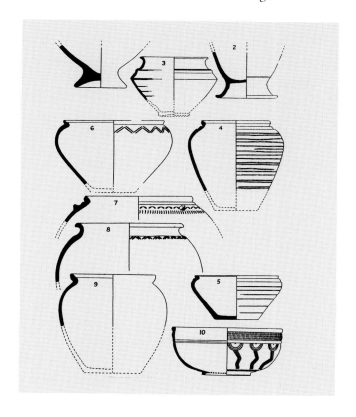

8   Removing the core earth during the investigation of the No.5 Denehole in 1887.

funerary urn, inverted and containing bones, was uncovered. The bones proved to be those of an adult and a child. Part of a quern (corn grinding stone) had been used as a base for the urn. An interesting find at this burial site was a faience bead, an indication of trading links with the continent. Thurrock is not short of examples of Iron-Age cultures. In 1955, at Hofford Wood Road at Linford, Iron-Age 'A' occupation finds included a large bucket, or 'situla' shaped vessel,

in coarse gritted ware. In February 1976 Barbara Jupp discovered a sherd of Iron-Age pottery near Stanford-le-Hope Creek, which an expert, Sheila Elsdon, identified as an example of La Tene-type decoration. Elsdon believed it came from a large pot, possibly akin to the globular omphalus-based pots found at Langenhoe and at Mucking. The colour is black to dark brown with a filler of very fine sand and quartzite elements.

During excavations for the A13 in 1979-80 a small Iron-Age settlement came to light 0.5km west of the Orsett enclosure and a similar distance north-west from the Orsett enclosure and its causeway. The settlement was sited on a hill of Boyn Hill Terrace (100ft. O.D.) with a scatter of small pits and postholes. An intriguing discovery was that one of them was a shallow bell-shaped storage pit, the floor of which was covered with carbonised wheat under several layers of backfilled clay and sand. Protected by the layers was an almost whole carimated jar of early Iron-Age type, together with large fragments of coarse flint-gritted pottery with finger impression decoration.

At West Thurrock in 1970, during gravel excavation in the Mill Lane Pit, several typically V-shaped ditches were revealed on a 100ft. gravel terrace. From the fill of the widest ditch came flint gritted sherds of pottery. At the time of excavation it was thought probable that the ditches represented field boundaries associated with the settlements of the Early Iron Age. The site appears to be part of a wider area of ancient occupation. Aerial photography has shown that a complex of prehistoric features exists to the north, nearer to the former Ardale Institution.

Many other finds from the Iron Age have occurred in Thurrock in addition to the important discoveries at the Mucking multi-period excavations. Iron-Age 'A' objects unearthed at Linford in the 1950s included a small pottery bowl and loom weights. A large urn of the period was discovered at Grays in 1920, and on another occasion a looped iron axe was also found at Grays. Iron-Age 'B' finds include pottery from an Aveley excavation of 1956 and a bowl dredged from the Thames at Grays. From the Late Iron-Age 'C' period (Belgic times) there are finds of pottery from the 1966 dig at Aveley and two vessels from Orsett; another from Stanford-le-Hope shows how rich the area is in Iron-Age archaeology. An unclassified Iron-Age find of two iron spearheads, also from the Thames, was made at Grays.

During the Iron Age (c.400-150 BC) it seems that settlements locally consisted of round tent-like houses or huts with shallow pits around them for drainage from the thatched roof; similar smaller huts were used for storage or cooking, and square wooden huts raised on four poles above the ground as granaries. Pits for storage and field ditches were also typical and good evidence for these has come from Rainham, just over the border

to the west of Aveley, as well as sites in Thurrock itself. It is believed that internal partitions divided the houses into daytime accommodation and sleeping areas. A hamlet of this type was occupied by a small group of families perhaps raising cattle and sheep for meat, milk, hides and wool. Barley and wheat crops would also be part of the farming scene. Clay loomweights and spindle whorls indicate weaving, while metal deposits may mean ironworking was practised. Iron ore was more widely available in the south-east than were copper and tin. These resources for the manufacture of weapons and tools were in full use by c.550 BC. They removed the dependency on ruling groups controlling metal obtainable only from a distance and led to a more equitable society.

The Celts and Rome

From c.300 BC the local republic of Rome began to expand its territory at a very fast rate. By 120 BC it was the sovereign power in Italy and began to spread its hegemony around the Mediterranean. The Celtic peoples to the north

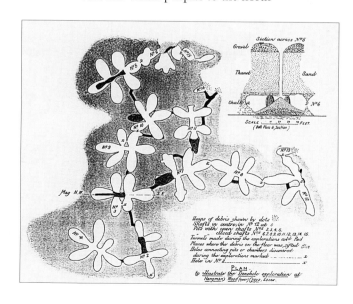

9 Plan of the Deneholes in Hangmans Wood. On the line of the Coal Road, they are thought to have been dug originally in prehistoric times. Various uses, from refuge against invaders, storage of grain and excavation of chalk and for lime, have been known over the centuries. The plan was made in 1887 when these pits were investigated by the Essex Field Club.

of the peninsula began sending the Roman Empire raw materials, food, slaves and mercenary troops. Political guarantees and luxury items flowed back to these peoples and a process of creeping Romanisation began even before the Romans expanded their rule northwards.

Various Roman influences had already made themselves felt at a distance. Celtic-style coins from Gaul (now France) first appeared in Britain c.200 BC with imported gold coins. The upper classes of society were soon using gold and silver coins for such things as bridal dowries. Regular shaped iron bars were also traded as a currency at the same time, for these could be converted into tools or weapons. A lower type of coinage came into use after 100 BC, manufactured from a tin-rich bronze known as 'potin', which seems to have been available for more straightforward transactions, such as when different peoples met at markets or tribal boundaries. Finds of these were fairly rare up to recent times, but in Thurrock they have been made both at Tilbury and Mucking, pointing to a prehistoric Thames crossing nearby. To the west of Thurrock the 19.4 hectare (48-acre) Uphall Camp site may also have provided a marketplace where different tribes could meet and 'potin' coins had been found there. This local trading centre seems to have been abandoned around 60 BC.

Just after this time the British tribes' support of a revolt against Roman rulers in Gaul brought Caesar to these shores: in August 55 BC he invaded with an army of 10,000, setting off from Boulogne and landing on the south coast near Deal. A battle on the beach left the British chiefs suing for peace. Following storm damage to his fleet Caesar had to spend time on repairs, and he withdrew again to France. In July 54 BC he returned with 25,000 infantry and 2000 cavalry together with supplies carried in over 800 ships. A successful landing drove the British back but storm damage again caused problems. However, the Roman force advanced across the Thames via a difficult but passable ford west of London. The British defenders had concealed pointed stakes in the bank and riverbed to defend themselves. Nevertheless the Roman cavalry and infantry were able to press forward together, overwhelming the British, who had united under a single military leader Cassivellaunus. The British, who retreated to his fortress at Wheathampstead, possibly included elements from Thurrock tribal groups.

Some natives surrendered and informed Caesar about the location of the British stronghold. Caesar then attacked and forced the British leader's surrender. Peace was agreed in exchange for hostages and an annual tribute to be delivered to Rome. Caesar sailed home satisfied. Britain had come into the Roman orbit and, although the Roman soldiers and administrators were not to return for almost a century, the shape of British society had changed. The smaller communities in Thurrock and elsewhere in the south east were uniting into larger tribes. The Trinobantes in our area and the Catuvellauni further west (both north of the Thames), with the Atrebates and Cantii to the south of the river, were the groups that faced up to later invaders.

A site at Chadwell St Mary was hurriedly investigated in 1959 before its destruction by gravel working. It showed signs of having been an Iron-Age settlement which continued on into the hundred years subsequent to the next Roman incursion, the Claudian invasion. The remains had been affected by ploughing over the centuries which had lowered the ground surface, obliterating signs of floors and walls.

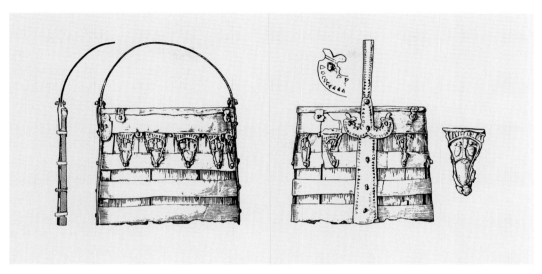

10 Details of a Saxon bronze-bound wooden bucket from Mucking.

There remained mostly 'V' section ditches and postholes in groups. The latter were suggestive of storage huts raised above ground on posts; the ditching suggested palisading and varied in width, but averaged seven feet, and was three feet in depth. Outside a boundary ditch were the remnants of a wooden coffin – with a larger number of chunky nails. Pottery from the site appeared to be first- and second-century Roman with some coarser ware, probably locally manufactured. Shards of Iron-Age 'A' pottery were thought to have been strays from further parts of the occupation area destroyed by gravel quarrying in the 1920s.

Romano-British occupation was widespread across Thurrock. During the A13 excavation in 1979-80, for instance, sites occupied over a period from the Iron Age to the Roman were revealed. At Belhus Park, on level terrain to the north of the Mardyke, aerial photographs showed two abutting rectangular enclosures. Pottery of the Early and Middle Iron Age was found; occupation in Late Iron-Age and Belgic

times was proved by increased finds of pottery and pieces of Belgic brick. Later ditches and pits and the discovery of Romano-British sherds are evidence of an active settlement in this area. In fact, a zone of settlements stretches across the district between sites at Rectory Road, Orsett, Baker Street, Stifford Clays, Ardale, William Edwards School and the Orsett Cock enclosure. The zone overlooks the Mardyke and Orsett Fen and enjoys a water supply from springs on the terrace slopes. It would have had good summer grazing and hunting grounds on the marshes.

A Romano-British cemetery discovered at the Mucking multi-period excavation site in 1978 contained 17 cremations and was the fourth cemetery of the period found there. The real surprise was a burial in a stone coffin with its lid, the body plaster wrapped on a wooden bier inside. The coffin had partially collapsed in the past but the remaining bones, the legs below the knees, suggested an adult male 25 to 35 years old. He must have been of some importance and wealth since the stone would have had to be imported: oolitic limestone occurs no nearer than the Oxford area and was brought along the River Thames. The Roman Army introduced burials in plaster into Britain, the practice having originated in the Mediterranean. This rare burial type was found among no fewer than four Romano-British cemeteries in Mucking from a total of 160 graves. The larger of two pots found in the grave pit had features which indicated a locally made necked jar with flattened rim. The jar, thought to date from the 4th century AD, placed this burial at a date a hundred years later than the other nearby cremations. It is fascinating to conjecture what it was that gave this man his important status.

Evidence of Roman farming has been found at Mucking among the later Saxon features. Near what is known as Well 4 were two different Romano-British buildings, the post pits of one suggesting an aisled barn and the other

11　A bronze-bound wooden bucket, from grave no. 600, of a male Saxon at Mucking.

resembling previously known wooden granaries from elsewhere. Other finds at Mucking included six Romano-British pottery kilns, and two Romano-British wells, which yielded wood from their rectangular lining and framing. Some of the rubbish dumped in Well 5 yielded numerous bronze scraps; a hairpin, needle, rivet, bangles and tweezers were recognisable. Pottery discovered carried second-century potters' stamps: Albucius, Banoluccus, Criciro, Lallus, Laxtucissa, Mercator, Musicus, Paulianus, Paullus, Senila and Tituro. The villa owners appear to have exercised their preferences in tastes, like modern consumers. A staple implement for Belgic and Romano-British inhabitants was the rotary quern and a good example has surfaced at Mucking.

A more luxurious item was a Romano-British flask with exceptional decoration found during gravel digging just east of the former Palmers Girls School in Little Thurrock. It came from a grave almost certainly connected with the local Roman settlement. R.A.H. Farrar of the Royal Commission on Historic Monuments believed the freehand design scored round the shoulder of the flask to be '3 genii cucullati', or hooded cult figures of a kind seen on religious sculptures. The Roman villa at Mucking must have had a high status given the kind of objects discovered on the site. A Roman amphora handle from an enormous jar used to transport wine, olive oil and fish paste gives us a glimpse of good living for the inhabitants. Other items include another handle, in the form of a woman's head, a bronze eagle's head vehicle mount from a cremation, and Samian ware vessels (the superior Roman pottery). A probable ritual pit here contained ten mica-dusted pottery lamps, nine coins, three tazza (pedestal cups), five colour coat beakers, eight pie dishes, and seeds of *pinus pinea*, the edible pine. It is difficult to visualise the rich and busy life of this villa in what is today a rather bleak Thamesside landscape. Mucking is a location for 4,000 years of settlement, which an excavation programme lasting more than a dozen years has explored in great detail. Its fame has spread abroad because of the new information gained on this shore about the Saxon lifestyle. Scholars from all over the world have studied the finds and knowledge won from the site, which did not get covered by an urban built landscape, and where various factors allowed the preservation and retrieval of so many original artifacts and landscape features.

In 1957 the evidence for Thurrock's Saxon connections was limited. It was known that at Linford Halls gravel pit had produced remains of Saxon settlements of two or more periods and that one site extended across the Hoford Road into adjoining fields, along the hundred-foot contour. There was another extension to Rainbow Shaw in the opposite direction. At Hall's Aveley pit a scatter of Saxon pottery was associated with a floor on this site. Lastly, West Tilbury provided an alleged location for Bishop Cedda's palace, west of the church. Pottery and loomweights from the Saxon period had been found at both the Linford and Aveley sites in 1955. A bronze bowl from a discovery at Tilbury in 1925 had gone to Southend Museum. The most prominent connection with Saxon times was through the local place-names (see Fig.1).

It was the archaeological excavation at the huge Mucking site from 1965 that showed how important the Saxon presence in Thurrock had

WEST TILBURY	735	*Tilaburga* (1000 – *Tilbuhere*)
ORSETT	957	*Aetorseapan*(1000 – *Orseapum*)
HORNDON	1042–66	*Horniduna*
GRAYS THURROCK	1066	*Turoca*
PURFLEET	1066	*Poerflotta*
AVELEY	1066	*Alvilea*
KENNINGTONS	1066	*Ketituna*
BELHUS PARK	1066	*Ramesduna*
OCKENDON (N & S)	1066	*Wochedona* (1086 – *Wokenduna*)
CHADWELL ST MARY	1066	*Celdwella*
STANFORD-LE-HOPE	1066	*Hasinbroc*
FOBBING	1068	*Fobbing(e)* (1086 – *Phobinge*)
STIFFORD	1086	*Estinfort* (*Stifort, Stiforda*)
LITTLE THURROCK AND WEST THURROCK	1086	*Tuocha* (*Thurrucca*)
BULPHAN	1086	*Bulgeuen* (1269 – *Bolegefanne*)
LANGDON HILLS	1086	*Langeduna*
CORRINGHAM	1086	*Currincham*
MUCKING	1086	*Mucinga*

Fig 1   *Derivation of modern place-names from Saxon English. The dates refer to the earliest known mention of the Saxon name.*

been. The site was complicated by the mass of evidence from different cultures over the thousands of years it had been occupied. Originally identified through aerial photographs which showed interesting crop marks, the jigsaw of features laid out on the landscape proved awe-inspiring. For instance, put end to end, the prehistoric ditches totalled seven km in length. Over 1,000 graves were found and 200 Saxon huts, a world record for a site. Different types of sunken hut were seen, Hut 110 being of unusual interest, having posts in each corner as well as the usual two to support a ridge pole. A German archaeologist, Ahrens, has classified it, the corner-post type, being more sophisticated in his typology than the gable-post type, the usual at Mucking. A shallow, narrow slot lying within the sunken area of Hut 110 provided the first obvious sign that some kind of wall, not necessarily stronger than a hurdle, was in some cases carried down to floor level in these huts. Hut 110 was of such interest to Saxon studies that during a Saxon Symposium in 1973 a busload of scholars from Denmark, France, Norway, Sweden, Germany, Holland and Hungary made a special visit. A ground-level Saxon 'hall', an early fifth-century claw-beaker and a sixth-century bronze-bound bucket all testify to the high status of the local Saxon community at this time.

Viking invaders destroyed Barking Abbey in the ninth century and Essex came under the jurisdiction of the Danelaw, a concentration of Danes even fortifying nearby Benfleet. In 912, however, Thurrock was freed from the Danelaw and in 920 a fortress was built by the Saxons at Maldon. The Saxon army which assembled to attack the Danish stronghold at Colchester may have included Thurrock men. The bloody Battle of Maldon in 991 marked the end of

the Danish wars, and a peace settlement was agreed between Edmund the Saxon and Cnut the Dane following the Battle of Ashingdon in 1016. Edward the Confessor used the nearby Palace of Havering while on the throne of England, but in 1066 his successor was defeated at the Battle of Hastings by William the Conqueror. The severity of the Norman yoke was felt strongly in Thurrock, which had been particularly loyal to King Harold.

William I was a harsh ruler who also had to keep his own Norman barons in order, but he was valued by the native English because he imposed law and order and stopped his barons stealing from or dealing unfairly with them. Before he died he ordered the compilation of the great Domesday record of 1086. Clerks were sent out to find out exactly how much each manor was worth, even detailing things like the number of ploughs, livestock and personnel. Thurrock communities included were Aveley, Stifford, Grays and West Thurrock, Little Thurrock, Chadwell, East and West Tilbury, Mucking and Orsett, divided between the hundreds of Chafford and Barstable. The survey suggests a largely pastoral community, with grazing for sheep and woodland for pigs, the exceptions being Mucking, West Thurrock and, especially, Orsett where there was more ploughland. It also notes how lands previously held by various freemen, servants of King Edward, bishops and priests were now in the hands of William's supporters such as the Bishop of London, the Bishop of Bayeux, William de Warenne and the Count of Eu.

In medieval times, most people in Thurrock were still unable to read or write. Most of the population spent their whole life in one village or small town community. Most citizens worked so hard on the land or in their specialised occupation within the feudal system that they had little energy or time for any other activity. For the majority of the population homes were very basic shelters, often crudely made from mud, wattle and daub. Cottages like these survived into the early 20th century in Orsett Road, Grays, for instance, and in the marshland villages of Thurrock. A type of medieval dwelling peculiarly adapted to Thurrock's marshland conditions has been discovered.

Randal Bingley has posited that the tide-washed wetlands of Corringham, Fobbing and Mucking were dotted with partly artificial mounds forming small islands on which homesteads were placed above the high tide level. These terp-mounds may date back to late prehistoric times and similar examples have been found in the wetland of Fahrstedter Wurth in East Friesland, and Feddersen Wierde in Germany. A Dutch excavation at the Ezing terp produced early Saxon pottery and loomweights similar to those found at the Mucking site. Many of these islands can be tentatively identified through place-names recorded in earlier documents. Area names with a 'worth' element are found across the Thurrock marshes and compare with the German (*werde*) and Dutch (*wierde*) names for these mounds. Instances are Slatey House at Fobbing, a former name of which was Westelward; Rugward marsh and homestead (Mucking); Wade Wyke of 1381 (Fobbing/Corringham); and Corringham's Radworth documented in 1199. The Roman Pliny the elder gives a description of such terpen (in this case in Germany), showing their persistence: 'Here a wretched race is found inhabiting either the more elevated spots of land or else eminences artificially constructed and of a height to which they know by experience tides will never reach, [where] they pitched

12 Turold of Rochester, the land grabber depicted on the Bayeux Tapestry.

their cabins and when the waves cover the surrounding country far and wide, twice a day, like so many mariners on board ship they are (detached from the land beyond).' One basis for such a mound can be identified just off the marshfoot at Fobbing, consisting of raised ash and salt crock briquetage after Early Iron-Age and Roman workers had evaporated saltwater to extract this valuable commodity.

Medieval churches were often brightly decorated and it was here that the people received not only religious instruction, but also relief from their toil; the music and colour possibly made their lives a little less drab at least once a week. Such a church existed at Grays, which seems to have been built originally in the first century after the Norman Conquest. A document confirms the church's existence in the 1150s, when it was granted to the order of Knights Hospitaller of St John of Jerusalem, but it was probably preceded by a manorial chapel which later formed the nucleus of the bigger church. This is implied by a document of 1086 which mentions Godwin of Thurrock, Chaplain. The colours of the priest's garb, and of the walls and windows, were expensive decorations, but the church was rich and powerful. Wealthy people acted as benefactors, making gifts to assuage their consciences over the ill-gotten gains that had made them rich. With life expectancy short, people were also mindful of buying credit that could be carried over into the kingdom of life after death.

The clerics were often the only learned men in the community. They wrote documents, letters and books of instruction, and their education made them the only people who understood the niceties of the law. Clerks outside the church were also required for drawing up legal agreements such as the transfers of land, property and administrative documents that kept the system running smoothly. An early document of 1199, the Confirmation of the Grant of the Manor of Thurrock to Henry de Gray, has survived. Translated from the Latin it reads:

John by the Grace of God, King of England, Lord of Ireland, Duke of Normandy, Count of Anjou. To the Archbishops, Bishops, Abbots, Counts, Barons, Justices, Viscounts, Sheriffs and all Bailiffs and faithful subjects; greeting, Know that we have granted and by this our present charter have confirmed to our beloved and faithful knight Henry de Gray the Manor of Thurrock with its appurtenances which belongs the fief of the Count de Ferrarus, on condition that he perform for the same Count what ought to be done for that Manor, on which condition he bought the same manor with its appurtenances from Josceus the son of Isaac, the Jew, to whom the same Count de Ferrarus by his charter had confirmed that manor when sold to him and his heir male Isaac. Wherefore we desire and confirm to the said Henry and his heirs after him the hereditament of the aforesaid manor with its appurtenances. Let them have and hold the manor-house in peace, freely and unmolested, in its entirety and honourably for the service which thence ought to be done for the Count

Confirmation of Grant to Henry de Gray by King John.

Johannes Dei gratia, Rex Angliae, Dominus Hiberniae, Dux Normandiae, Comes Andjou, Archiepiscopis Episcopis, Abbotibusi Comitibus, Baronibus, Justiciis, Vicecomitibus, Prepositis et omnibus Baillivis et fidelibus suis Salutem Sciatis nos concessisse et present, carta nostra confirmasse dilecto et fideli militi nostro Henrico de Gray manerium de Turroc cum pertinentibus suis quod est de feodo comitis de Ferrarus ut idem faciat eidem comiti quod de manerio illo fieri debet dehoc emit idem manerium cum pertinentibus suis de Josceo filio Isaac Judeo cui idem Comes de Fyrarus illud manerium venditum sibi et primogenito suo Isaac carta sua confirmaverat Quare volumus et firmamus precipuum quod dictus Henricus et heredes sui post eum predictum manerium cum pertinentibus suis Habeant et teneant burgum et inpace libere et quiete integritate plenarie et honorfice per servicium quod inde fieri debet Comiti de Ferrarus in omnibus locis et rebus ad id manerium pertinentibus cum omnibus libertatibus et liberis consuetudinibus suis et cum omni integritate sua sic carta Regis Ricardi fratris nostri et Comitis de Ferrarus quas inde hi testant. Testibus: S. Bathonis Episcopo; Willelmo Comite Arundell; R. Comite de Meullent; Willelmo filio Radolfi, Seniore Normandiae: Roberto filio Walteri; Rogero Constabulario Cestri. Datum per manum H. Cantuaraburgi Archiepiscopi Cancellarii nostri apud Veruelamium xxvi. die July, Anno regni nostri primo.

13   The Latin wording of Henry de Gray's grant from King John. The family name added a Norman epithet to an original Saxon place description (Grays Thurrock).

de Ferrarus in all places and matters pertaining to that manor with all its liberties and free customs and in all its entirety as under the charter of our brother King Richard and of the Count de Ferrarus which these witness. Witnesses: S. Bishop of Bath, William Count Arundel, R. Count Meullent, William Fitz- Radolph, a knight of Normandy, Robert Fitz-Walter, Roger Constable of Chester. Given under the hand of H. Archbishop of Canterbury, Our Chancellor at St Albans on the twenty sixth day of July in the first year of Our Reign.

From seven fragments of the Grays manorial accounts of different dates between 1290 and 1433, which were discovered in a south London junk dealer's cellar in November 1986, it seems that the manor was a thriving and successful business under the de Grays, making a profit of £175 for the year 1302, a sizeable one for the time. The Essex Record Office reported that the manor appears to have been practically self-sufficient. Few provisions were brought in from elsewhere, except wine and some fish and almonds to feed the household at Lent. Livestock included cattle, pigs, sheep, oxen, carthorses, doves, hens, capons and geese. Cereals grown included barley, wheat, mixed corn and rye. Sales from the estate involved wool, fells (sheep skins with wool attached) and willows.

The trade in sheep and sheep products was important in the area in the Middle Ages. Fobbing, for instance, had pasturage for 700 sheep in the time of Count Eustace's tenure. The wide marshes facing the Thames provided grazing for thousands of the animals, which were a key feature of the local economy. The level of prosperity was shown by the building of houses like Larkins at Orsett in the late 15th century. This still stands proudly at a rural road junction and is a timber-framed cottage of some

14 The fine Flemish brass of Ralph de Knevynton (modern Kenningtons) in Aveley church. He died in 1370. The depiction with pointed hauberk owes more to the Cyclas period of armour than the Camail period in which he was active.

distinction that any well-off yeoman would have been proud to own.

In Aveley in the same century the Cely family were celebrated wool merchants. The head of the family, Richard, died in late 1481 or early 1482 leaving three sons, Richard, Robert and George. Richard and George continued in the trade, Richard living at Bretts Place in Aveley. A relative, William Cely, was agent in Calais where a centre of the wool trade known as the Staple was set up after the town was captured from the French. In the Cely Papers, William Midwinter

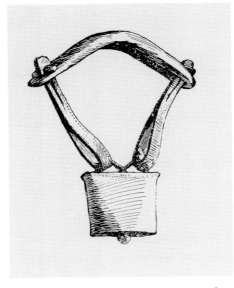

15 Sheep bells found on the marshes of Tilbury parishes remind us of the great numbers that grazed here in the Middle Ages. A local market was held on the marshes and sheep were brought over the river from Kent and Sussex.

is often mentioned as someone who sells wool to the Celys. This wool travelled by packhorse from other parts of England, some, for instance, across the Wiltshire and Hampshire Downs, then through Surrey and Kent to the ports there. Suffolk and Essex also provided wool, which could be transported across the Thames from Tilbury to Gravesend and then to Sandwich and on by ship to Calais. Some ships even sailed from Rainham, east of Purfleet, with Essex cargoes of wool and Essex cheese on board bound for Calais. Following the capture of the French port in 1346 the Staple of Calais was devised as a market and entrepôt so that Essex wool sent to France could be bought, sold and taxed.

For over 400 years, a sheep and cattle fair was held in the neighbourhood of Tilbury Fort. Essex

farmers and dealers bought stock here which they then fattened to provide a supply for the London and Essex markets. Presumably some of these beasts had been brought across the Thames from Kent. An old house on West Tilbury Common, in the middle of nowhere, was built to be used as an alehouse, possibly to slake the thirsts of these traders, but it was never licensed. A 14th-century manorial document mentions the names of Will Catton and Thomas Porter of Aveley as holders of the rights to three acres of marsh and pasture to sustain a flock of 24 sheep at Stanford-le-Hope. For this they paid a 'quit' rent of a cock and two hens as well as providing other services to the lord of the manor. Still standing today, the wool market at Horndon-on-the-Hill is a survivor of wool-trading times. Sales still took place here in the 19th century, when there were wool fairs in June and July. Repairs to the floor of this hall in the 20th century revealed a number of Dutch coins which had dropped through small cracks, reminders of the Dutch men who built the sea walls on Canvey and the marshmen from the Island who carried their wool and other items to Horndon.

Essex clothmakers had a good reputation for honest trading. An Act of Parliament of 1390 regulating clothmaking promulgated that: 'All cloth sold in English fairs and markets is to be

16 A Saxon glass horn from a rich burial at Rainham, the next Saxon settlement along the Thames from Purfleet. This was part of a group of items found in 1937 originating from a wealthy ruling group.

opened out in the roll so that buyers at home and abroad can see the quality … as is done in the County of Essex.' Artefacts from the West Tilbury marshes donated to the Thurrock Museum include several relics connected with Henry Cole of 'Condovers'. These included iron sheep bells complete with their leather and wooden yokes and branding irons bearing the owner's 'H.C.' mark. The irons were not used hot, as on horses and cattle, but were used to apply red paint known as 'riddle', an ironstone pigment.

In 1381 another event of national import involved local rebels against the Poll Tax. Jack Straw, one of the principal leaders, was believed to have been the priest serving Fobbing church. The revolt is supposed to have occurred when a new tax commissioner, Thomas Bampton, demanded tax from poverty-stricken local fishermen from Stanford-le-Hope, Corringham and Fobbing. Apparently, the previous winter the commissioners had understood the locals' plight and had let them off from payment. All over Essex, Kent and London men tried to throw off the yoke of harsh lords. At first, King Richard appeared to accept many of their demands. But the forces of civil disorder saw John Ewell beheaded at Langdon Hills and many other scores settled, murder, pillage and an inevitable clampdown of law and order eventually leading to trials and executions. Thus ended an early local revolt against a feudal order which could not easily cope with changing social conditions.

In 1510, Margaret, daughter of Hugh Shaa of a famous local family in Horndon-on-the-Hill, married Thomas Rich of an even more famous line (Lord Rich, a relation, was Lord Chancellor to Queen Elizabeth I). Margaret's grandson was Edward Rich of Horndon. He it was who apparently entertained Elizabeth when she visited the grand camp of 1,000 horse and 22,000 foot at West Tilbury on the occasion of the approach to these shores of the Spanish Armada. The Earl of Leicester staged a mock battle on the extended plateau above the Thames. One of Thurrock's most glorious historic events was crowned by the famous speech which reverberated across Europe and summarised the credo of Elizabeth's reign: 'I am come amongst you, not for my recreation and disport, but being resolved, in the midst and heat of battle, for my God and for my Kingdom, and for my people, my honour and my blood, even in the dust. I know I have the body of a weak and feeble woman, but I have the heart and stomach of a King.' Today her visit to 'Campe Royall' is still remembered by the inclusion of the Tudor Rose in Thurrock's coat of arms.

TWO

Grays: From Little Port to Growing Town

∽≋∾

The successful management of their town by the de Grays in the Middle Ages seems to have led to general prosperity from this time. In the town's favour was the advantage of having both a market and a port. An ancient custom had been established called 'Purveyance', which enabled the Crown to purchase farm stock and dairy produce at below the local price and market value. This had the effect of making those markets chosen by the Royal Commissioners – Grays Thurrock and Romford – into efficient bulk suppliers. The Commissioners specified that over 1,000 lambs and sheep should be supplied weekly and delivered through these markets to the court gates, or 'wherever the Crown may direct'. Apart from this, great consignments of game, poultry and dairy produce were also purchased from Grays. The easiest way to get produce to London was by water; the road connections were not half as convenient, although some loads were despatched by road. The figures prove the popularity of despatch by river from Grays, the town being the main river port in south-west Essex, where exports were valued at £250,000 – an unbelievable sum for medieval times.

The origin of Grays market was a charter of Henry III (*c.*1220). This was later confirmed by Edward II in 1330. Richard de Gray gained the right to hold a market on Fridays, together with a fair on 28/29 June each year. By the 19th century there were two fair days: 23 May and 20 October. Pepys mentions Grays Market in his diary for 5 April 1660: 'at night Mr Shepley overtook us, who had been at Grays market this morning.' Pepys was often about his business and pleasure on the river Thames, and another reference occurs on 24 September 1665 (Lord's day):

> Waked, and up and drank, and then to discourse; and then being about Grayes, and a very calme, curious morning we took our wherry, and to the fishermen, and bought a great deal of fine fish, and to Gravesend to White's, and had part of it dressed.

On 10 June 1667 a Dutch fleet got into the Thames and there was much alarm, so Pepys wrote:

> Up; and news brought us that the Dutch are come up as high as the Nore; and more pressing orders for fire ships … Here [Greenwich] I was with much ado fain to press two watermen to make me a galley and so to Woolwich to give order for the dispatch of a ship I have taken under my care to see dispatched, and orders being so

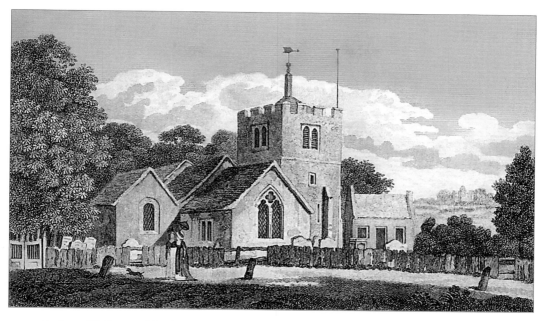

17 A view of St Peter and Paul, Grays in 1807, which shows the church's much altered appearance at that time. The original Palmer's School was in the building to the right of the picture. A Charter of the 1150s grants it to the Knights Hospitaller of St John.

given, I, under pretence to fetch up the ship, which lay at Grays (the *Golden Hind*), did do that in my way, and went down to Gravesend where I find the Duke of Albemarle just come, with a great many idle lords and gentlemen, with their pistols and fooleries; and the bulwarke not able to have stood half an hour had they come up; but the Dutch are fallen down from the Hope and Shellhaven as low as Sheernesse, and we do plainly at this time hear the guns play.

The *Ambulator*, or 'a pocket companion for the tour of London and Its Environs' (11th edition, 1811) dismisses Grays in a few words: 'A market town in Essex. The town is small but pleasantly situated on the side of a hill. Its market house is a good building, on which is a large session-room, where the petty sessions are held … Grays market is held on Thursday.' A better

summary of the town is given by William White in his publication of 1848:

Grays Thurrock is a small ancient town on the north bank of the river Thames, twenty and a half miles E. by S. of Whitechapel, and 4 miles N. W. by W. of Gravesend. It has a small creek or harbour, which receives hoys and other vessels as large as 300 tons; and has a wooden pier, 400 feet long, constructed in 1841, at the cost of 2,500, by a company of proprietors, in £10 shares. The London and Gravesend steam vessels call at the pier five times a day, and the town presents a scene of considerable traffic, especially in bricks and tiles, of which large quantities are made here, and sent to London. Here are also extensive lime quarries, in which many curious fossils are found. The town has likewise a large brewery, and a coast guard consisting of a captain and seven men. It had formerly a corn market every

18 Looking from the market down the High Street towards the level crossing. Ffrench's Restaurant on the right is above Saxton's the tobacconist's shop. Kentex, the dry cleaners, part of a chain, has the shop at 81 beyond Saxton's. An informal meeting and exchange of gossip is taking place in front of the church wall on the left.

Thursday, but it declined after the institution of that at Romford, about 30 years ago … Its parish contains 1,332 acres of land and had only 677 inhabitants in 1801; but in 1831, they had increased to 1,248, and in 1841 to 1,464 souls. It received the distinguishing part of its name from the noble family of Grey, who held it more than three centuries … It was held by his family till 1521, as parcel of the Duchy of Lancaster and honor of Mandeville. James Theobald Esq. is now lord of the manor and owner of most of the soil. Belmont Castle, the delightful seat of Richd. Webb, Esq., belongs to Geo. R. Hilliard and stands half a mile W. of the town on the summit of an eminence which rises abruptly from the banks of the Thames. It was built by the late Zachariah Button Esq., who finished in a costly style of architecture. The centre is a round embattled tower, in four storeys, with spacious apartments commanding extensive prospects of the river, the shipping, and the rich Kentish enclosures, to the hills beyond the great Dover road. The pleasure grounds are tastefully disposed and ornamented with trees and shrubs of great value and of beautiful forms. The church (St Peter and St Paul) was rebuilt by the parishioners in 1846, at the cost of £1,800, on its original cruciform plan and in the Anglo-Norman style. The tower has three bells and is crowned by a small spire. James Theobald Esq. is patron, and the Revd H.S. Hele, M.A., is the incumbent and has a neat residence, but no glebe … The old Town Hall was converted into an independent chapel in 1836; and there is a small Wesleyan Chapel built in 1837. Here are several Sunday Schools and an endowed Charity School. In 1706, Wm.

Palmer vested in trust for the foundation of a Charity School and other charitable uses in this parish, five tenements in Whitecross street, and one in Lombard street, London. Part of this property was sold in 1786 for £600, which was invested in the purchase of £944 12s. 6d. three per cent Consols. The property in London now belonging to the charity consists of the houses numbered 218 and 220 Whitecross street, and that numbered 43 in Lombard street. These houses are let for about £100, which added to the stock, swells the yearly income to the charity to about £140. By his will in 1709, the donor gave the school and master's house. The master has a yearly salary of £70, and is required to teach 20 poor boys as free scholars; and four of them are

clothed by the trustees at the annual cost of £9. Five chaldron of coals are annually distributed, one to the Charity School and the other four to about 65 poor families. The sum of £1 per annum is applied in monthly doles of bread; and £1 for a sermon on the 5th of November. The founder directed that the surplus income should be liable to the repairs of the parish causeway, and to a yearly allowance of 40 shillings for the entertainment of the churchwardens and overseers on the 5th of November when they should meet to enquire into the management of the charity. Sir T.B. Lennard, his four sons, and others were appointed trustees in 1818. The poor parishioners had the interest of £14 derived from the gift of a Mr Brandon. They had

a yearly rent of £4, left by Wm. Hansworth, in 1759, out of four houses; but the owner (Mr J.H. Brand) refused to pay it in 1834, alleging that it was void by the statute of Mortmain.

In 1847 the Grays post office was 'at Thomas Hewers', a draper in the town, and letters were despatched at 4 o' clock. William Palmer, who had founded the famous school, was a J.P. and lord of the manor. A widower who had no children, it seems he may have wanted to give something back to the town as he neared the end of a long life. The trust he set up did not insist that the school bear his name, but was extremely business-like, laying down specifically how the

19 An entrance to Palmer's School about 1929.

20 A popular shop in New Road, Grays, Lanham and Pennington specialised in uniforms for local schools. Incomes were generally low in the 1950s and many could not afford even sale prices but had to make do with other people's cast-offs and the charity of relatives.

12 trustees who were to administer the revenue were to be appointed. Palmer also set down details for the construction of a schoolroom, and a site for this was given. Great care was taken in both the Trust Deed and Palmer's Will to provide a solid foundation and this resulted in the survival of the school through the 18th, 19th and 20th centuries, unlike many other such foundations which suffered from poorly financed or administered funds. An early mention in the 19th century occurs in a letter from Matthew Wilson, vicar of Grays, to the Archdeacon of Essex: 'There is a free Charity School for boys;

the number twelve … other boys attend the school, but they pay for their education once a quarter'. By 1864 the school had 109 pupils, 41 being educated free as Foundation Scholars.

Belmont Castle is interesting in that it represents the ambition of *nouveaux riches* entrepreneurs in Essex to own or build a mansion which would add prestige to economic success. H.E. Brooks, in his book on Palmer's School, wrote of the entrepreneur Zachariah Button that he

> followed his father in the occupation of Mucking Hall and with money made by farming, seized

21 Children with play hoops in Whitehall Road.

22   Grays Thurrock United were an ambitious football team, members of which are seen here in about 1927. Second on the right in the back row is Chris Edmondson.

23   A Grays F.C. match in progress on the Recreation Ground has attracted male and female supporters. The houses and buildings of Bridge Road are seen beyond the ground.

24 The newcomer to Grays in the early 20th century would have found the High Street provided a good choice of shopping and also entertainment. The Empire Theatre, originally a variety theatre, had just started showing films. National multiples were beginning to augment those more locally-based firms.

every opportunity of acquiring land in the neighbourhood. In 1777 he purchased Peverill manor of Grays from Sir John Van Hattem who had inherited it from the widow of the second Sir Thomas Davall, and about 1795, he built Belmont and surrounded it by the park which in my younger days extended right down on to the London Road.

This residence, no doubt, helped to establish Button as an even more solid citizen, and he became Deputy Lieutenant for Essex and also a Sheriff.

A later owner was Richard Webb, who became a trustee of Palmer's School, and the house under him was described by Wright in 1836:

The building, beside other convenient apartments, contains ... an elegant drawing-

25 Market day in the 1950s on the corner of New Road and High Street, by the church. A corner of Joyes Department Store can be seen on the left.

room, measuring twenty feet by eighteen, with a circular front, richly ornamented; and a library-room, fitted up in the most elegant manner; from this apartment a double flight of stone-steps descend to the terrace, fronting the great lawn, and in full view of the river. Lofty walls surround a very extensive kitchen-garden, with a capital hot-house, and a choice selection of the best fruit-trees. Surrounding the house are the pleasure-grounds, which are tastefully disposed, and ornamented with forest-trees, of great value and of beautiful forms: shrubs and plants terminated toward the west by a gothic temple, and toward the east by an orchard and paddock. There are two approaches to the house; the one by a neat, brick gothic lodge, through the great south lawn, from the road between West Thurrock and Grays; and the other from the village of Stifford, by the north lawn.

On one side of this Gothic folly were the four chalk pits of Grays and on the other (western) side increasing industrial activity and mineral extraction. In the town itself tramways ran down to the wharves carrying wagons filled with the harvest of the pits; Grays own industrial revolution had been proceeding apace, making several businessmen and entrepreneurs wealthy. On the Thames barges carried off chalk, whiting and bricks to destinations near and far. Business was good for the public houses and other services provided by old Grays High Street, with its higgledy-piggledy collection of buildings from different centuries tumbling down towards the wharves. A whole world was swept away with its destruction towards the end of the 20th century.

26 Joyes ladieswear department on the Market Square, Grays advertised Easter 1930 offerings to the fashionable ladies of the district. This local department store was waking up to the value of newspaper advertising.

Orsett: An Important Centre

Orsett still has the air of being detached from nearby towns and suburbs – it is characteristic of parts of Essex that have survived into the modern era. One reason is the presence around the village of a great number of attractive trees with open fields and meadows beyond. North of the village stretches the open fen, with its great breadth of sky above. The manor was at one time the property of the Bishops of London, but Elizabeth seized it for the Crown in 1558. It was removed from the infamous Bishop Bonner, the remains of whose supposed palace are still faintly visible in the form of mounds in the village, by an Act of Parliament. The manor was leased by the Queen

27 (*top*) Some of the goods available at Horncastles Stores, Grays in 1930. The wire netting was useful for people intending to keep chickens to supplement their food. Chicken coops lined the yards or gardens of many local houses and cottages.

28 (*above*) 'Bishop Bonner's Palace' at Orsett in the 1930s. This term really applies to various ruined mounds in the vicinity. The house is known as Old Hall Farm.

29   The Southend Road at Socketts Heath in the 1950s. The population of the area was rising. Some car owners have parked and are picnicking on the verges of Hangmans Woods.

to William Holdstocke, at one time Comptroller of the Navy, who contributed handsomely to the erection of Orsett's church tower.

The old country crafts were still practised in the village up to the 20th century. In the

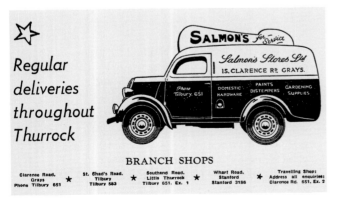

30   Salmon's van. Travelling shops and delivery vans of various kinds were common in the first half of the 20th century.

smithy were displayed not only horseshoes but also the oxshoes used on plough oxen, famous for their steady pull and the way their hooves created a fine tilth in the course of their progress over the fields. Orsett thatchers were famous for their work on cottages in the village and for miles around. Orsett always had an influential role in the areas round about. The Orsett Estate stretched over many acres and was famous in the 19th and 20th centuries for introducing improved farming methods. The Orsett Show, a shop window for farming practice and the countryside, began in the 19th century and continues up to the present day.

The *Whitmore Arms*, at a crossroads in the village, commemorates a family who have been lords of the manor. Sir Francis Whitmore, who died in 1962 at the age of 91, had a long and distinguished career in both the civilian

31 New Road, seen here in Edwardian times, was quite an important shopping street. Many of the shops, including Davies the tailor in the distance, were small local concerns and there were still houses on the left-hand side.

and military arenas. From 1916 to 1918 he commanded the Essex Yeomanry, and from 1918 to 1919 the Royal Hussars. In 1917 he was awarded the DSO, in the following year he was made a Companion of the Order of St Michael and St George, and in 1935 a Companion of the Bath award followed. His services during the Second World War earned him a knighthood. He was Lord-Lieutenant of Essex from 1936.

William White says of Orsett in 1848:

A large and pleasant village 9 miles S. by W. of Billericay, five and a half miles N. of Tilbury Fort, and 12 miles E.S.E. of Romford, gives name to the large Union (for workhouse purposes). Its parish comprises 1390 inhabitants, and 4136 acres of land, including the village of Baker Street, about a mile W. of the church; but exclusive of a detached member called Orsett hamlet which has 45 inhabitants, and is distant 13 miles north of Orsett, being in Chelmsford Hundred,

and comprising a considerable parcel of land, between the parishes of Buttsbury, Stock and Margaretting, belonging to Lord Petre, and anciently forming Crondon Park, which was divided into farms many years ago. This hamlet is only connected ecclesiastically with Orsett, and pays a yearly modus of £16 to the rector in lieu of tithes ... About one and a half miles N.W. of the village is Orsett Fen, where there is a stinted common of about 200 acres ... Mrs Baker is now lady of the manor of Orsett, but the greater part of the parish belongs to W. and R.B. Wingfield, Col. Bonham, S. Newcombe, and several smaller proprietors. Orsett Hall is a large and ancient mansion, which belonged to the Bishops of London till the reign of Elizabeth, when it passed with the manor to the Crown. James I granted it to Francis Downes, but in 1650 it passed to John Hatt. In 1746, it was sold by the trustees of Richd. Letchmere to Richd. Baker. Near it are the remains of a moat, and in the parish are several other good houses, one of

which is Orsett House, a respectable boarding school. The manor of Sabur, or Seborow, extends into this parish and those of Mucking and Chadwell, and anciently belonged to St Mary's Hospital, without Bishopsgate, London; and here is another estate called Lost Hall which has been held by the Baesh, Parker and Downes families. And was anciently the endowment of a chantry in the Bishop's Palace, London. The Church (St Giles and All Saints) is a large and ancient structure, consisting of a nave with aisles, a chancel, with north and south chapels, and

a brick tower, crowned by a wooden spire. It is in good repair, and had formerly a chantry, founded by Thomas Hotoft. It has several neat monuments; and in the chapel belonging to Orsett Hall is a handsome one, in memory of John Hatt, who died in 1658. The rectory valued in K.B. at £29 6s. 8d., and in 1831 at £812, is in the patronage of the Bishop of London, and the incumbency of the Revd James Blomfield, who has about nine acres of glebe, and a handsome residence built in the Elizabethan style. The tithes have been commuted for £1,225.

32 W. Cockley's festive refreshment stall at the Recreation Ground on a sports day about 1920. R. White's Kaola drink was an imitation of American brands.

Here is an Independent Chapel, and the parish has National, Infant, and Diocesan schools and various Charities for the poor. PARISH LANDS etc. In 1495 Thomas Hotoft gave to the parishioners of Orsett for their general benefit, about 40 acres of land, now let for £60 a year, the whole of which has been applied in aid of the poor rates since 1834, previous to which a portion of the rent was distributed in bread, at Christmas and Easter. About 8 and a half acres of land, called Slade's Hold, was given to the parishioners by an unknown donor and was let in 1801 for 40 years at £5 per annum; the lessee giving a bonus of £200 which was laid out towards building the Workhouse, which stands on part of the said land, and has since been appropriated to the use of Orsett Union at the yearly rent of £20. This rent and that of the land are carried to the account of Orsett poor rates. The Charity School, where 14 boys are educated and clothed, was built in 1776 by Edward Anson, who endowed it with Epping Farm at Theydon Garnon, which contains 23 acres, and is now let for £30 a year … The master occupies the school house and has a salary of £20. The 14 free scholars are provided with books and are clothed at about £43 per annum. When there is a sufficient surplus, apprentice fees of £10 10s. each are given with one or two of the most deserving scholars. The Rector, Sir T.B. Lennard, the Vicar of Horndon-on-the-Hill, and others are the trustees. The 14 free scholars are chosen as follows; six from the parish of Orsett, and two each from the parishes of Horndon-on-the-Hill, Bulphan, Mucking, and Chadwell, agreeable to the founder's will.

Orsett was situated in the Barstable Hundred and William White describes Orsett's function as one of the Workhouse Unions in the Hundred:

> Orsett Union comprises the 18 parishes of Aveley, Bulphan, Chadwell, Corringham, Fobbing, Horndon-on-the-Hill, Laindon Hills, Mucking, North and South Ockendon, Orsett, Stanford-le-Hope, Stifford, Grays Thurrock, Little and West Thurrock, and East and West Tilbury – which embrace an area of 65 square miles, and had 10,157 inhabitants in 1841, consisting of 5,361 males and 4,796 females, living in 1697 houses, besides which there were 33 unoccupied, and 3 building, when the census was taken. The total average annual expenditure on the poor of the 18 parishes during the three years preceding the formation of the Union, was £5,605, but in 1838 it amounted only to £3,954, and in 1840 to £4,702. The Union Workhouse is at Orsett and has room for 200 paupers. It was built in 1837, at the cost of £3,115. Mr Henry Robinson and Mrs Sarah Jackson are the master and matron. Mr North Surridge, of Romford, is the Union Clerk and Superintendant Registrar; and Mr John Crisp Boggis is the relieving officer.

In later years the Orsett Union authorities had problems dealing with the outbreak of infectious diseases such as smallpox at the increasingly important port of Tilbury which had developed

33 (*above*)   Orsett High Road in the 1940s. Entrance to the church is on the right. The Post Office has been a movable feature, also migrating to the other side of the road.

34 (*below*) Looking at the village from the opposite direction in the 1920s, complete with a vintage car.

within Chadwell parish. The outbreaks had to be contained and accurate figures obtained of cases and outcomes, putting a great strain on the officials of a supposedly rural authority. The Grays overseers of the poor had leased an old public house, *The Green Man and Bell*, as their workhouse.

On 19 December 1872 the Orsett Rural Sanitary Authority met for the first time, with the Revd John Windle as chairman. He was succeeded by C. Asplin and Samuel W. Squier by 1880. In 1886, when the Revd T. Crawley was chairman, Grays Thurrock was hived off and formed into a separate Local Board of Health authority. In July 1887 it was reported that the hospital administration buildings had been completed. In 1888 there was an outbreak of typhoid which was the subject of a detailed report from the Medical Officer of Health. The last meeting of the Rural Sanitary Authority was held on 20 December 1894. The new Orsett Rural District Council's early meetings were not recorded accurately because only brief notes were made, but it appears that in May 1899, when Mr Champion Russell was elected chairman, meetings were held at Tilbury in a shop facing the Dock Station, and this arrangement continued for some time. The council was constantly facing problems owing to subsidence affecting the pipes of the first sewerage scheme laid in the marshy subsoil.

Soon Chadwell St Mary parish informed the Rural District Council that they were to apply for the formation of an urban district. Orsett RDC did not oppose the application and from this time the sway of the Orsett officials was in decline. However, they continued to work on various schemes, with Grays UDC on the management of the Grays Isolation Hospital, for example, on

35 A peaceful stretch of the Southend Road, Grays, near Palmer's School about 1912. Mrs Emily Watson's grocer's shop at 7 Southend Road may have provided sweets for passing scholars who had a farthing or halfpenny to spare.

private street works, control of smallpox (there were 73 cases in January 1902, most of whom had not been vaccinated, and 14 Deaths), and on sewerage work for Stanford-le-Hope, at a cost of £7,500. Chadwell parish's attempt to form a new council to deal with the problems arising from the growth and development of Tilbury town led to the birth, on 1 April 1912, of Tilbury Urban District Council.

Orsett soldiered on. In May 1915, on the motion of the Revd C.J.H. Llewellyn, business was suspended while a prayer was offered up for the nation in this time of trouble. In August 1917 the Orsett Food Control Committee was inaugurated, shortly after it was decided to acquire sites for the purpose of housing provision, there being a great shortage in the area. In 1926 it was resolved to borrow £74,250 to provide

housing for the working classes and the decision was taken to build 200 houses in November of that year. The following year Orsett applied to the Ministry for permission to construct a further 200 homes, after it had completed one contract in West Thurrock. In 1928 the Council sought to raise a loan of £54,000 for houses in Corringham, Horndon-on-the-Hill and Stanford-le-Hope. In the following years application was made for a loan of £10,640 for around 65 acres in Little Thurrock for a playing field, and for a joint sewerage scheme for Corringham, Horndon and Stanford, but a Review of Districts was being undertaken at the time. The final meeting of Orsett Rural District Council took place on 12 March 1935.

Orsett at one stage had a very successful Quoits team which won one of the prestigious

36 New Road about 1912 provided services such as a carpenter and joiner and specialist shops.

37 The top end of Bridge Road, a smart residential area in 1912.

38 A large force of policemen on duty at Grays in July 1912 to forestall possible outbreaks of trouble during a strike.

trophies: the Taylor Walker shield was a wonderful silver object five feet high and three feet wide. Quoits was one of the most popular pastimes in Essex in Victorian times and right up to the First World War. It was played with a steel ring which was thrown from about twenty yards on to steel rods fixed in circles approximately three feet apart. The venues for these games were rural public houses and inns which in those days opened all day from 6 a.m. to midnight. Parties of players and supporters travelled by coach along country byways to attend matches. Orsett dominated the game for several years.

One of the great players from the village was William Kempster, who won the National Quoit Championship of Great Britain in 1895, 1896 and 1911, and also the News of the World Challenge Cup, the Gamage Silver Bowl, the Sporting Life trophy and the Essex Challenge Cup, which, together, show what a widespread interest was taken in the sport by all. The *Foxhounds* at Orsett, the *Bull Inn*, Corringham, the *Ship*, Little Thurrock, the *Cross Keys*, Chadwell St Mary, *Wharf Inn*, Grays and the *Harrow*, Bulphan all had excellent pitches.

THREE

The River Thames

❦

Objects found in the area prove that the Thames has been a means of communication with other parts of the world since prehistoric times. A recent find of rich Saxon burial objects, many made out of gold, led one archaeologist to comment that 'you can draw arrows from all over Europe and the near east tracing the origin of the goods found here'. In modern times, before the coming of the steamship, large numbers of sailing barges were used on the river. In the 19th and early 20th centuries a number of wharves in the Grays area dealt particularly with the products of the chalk workings and brickfields of the town, but many other commodities were landed and

39 Small sailing craft seen off the shore at Purfleet in about 1920. In earlier centuries quite small craft made hazardous trips across the seas and oceans.

40 A 17th-century East Indiaman, one of a fleet which was seen on the Thames. The East India Company received its charter from Queen Elizabeth I. From the Middle Ages ships grew larger and capable of carrying ever more valuable cargoes.

taken away; with the rise of retail food shops, for example, the Grays Co-operative Society had its own wharf. There was a prosperous coastwise trade down the eastern side of England. Coal, a vital fuel used both by domestic and industrial customers, was brought from the coalfields of north-east England in great quantities. This trade dated back several centuries. A landmark in the Thurrock area was the Tilbury hailing station on the banks of the Thames, which could transmit information to the London docks from coal vessels sailing up the river. It is interesting to note that the *Dictionary of the Thames* of 1880,

compiled by Charles Dickens, records a sailing barge fleet on the Thames of no fewer than 3,000 vessels. By 1885 2,100 sailing barges were officially registered, a figure that remained steady up to 1910 and only declined after that date. Before the Second World War there were still nearly 10,000 barges on the river carrying many types of cargo.

The Thames has been called the greatest industrial seaway in the world, yet along the Thurrock reaches the river also has a mystery and charm that wind, tide and weather together create. The ever-changing and atmospheric scene

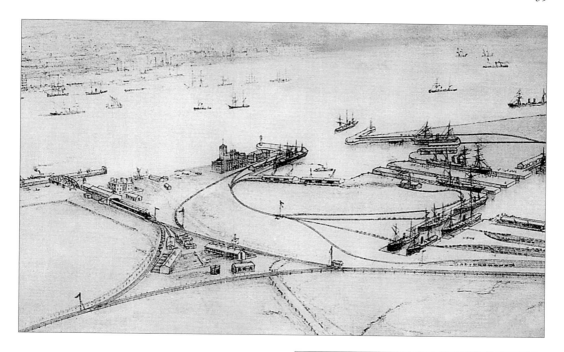

41 (*top*)   Tilbury Docks railway system, 1886.

42 (*right*)   The opening of the Docks.

43 (*below right*)   The basin, Tilbury Docks, about 1912. It was a popular activity for those on holiday to go and see the large steamships arriving and departing.

calls up memories of the river's long history; from a time when the Phoenicians rowed their galley up to Canvey and Thurrock, bringing cargoes of precious metals and other exotic trading goods, to the sudden rise of Tilbury Docks and new links with the rest of the world. With the construction of the Tilbury landing stage Thurrock welcomed the great days of liner travel, when rich voyagers stayed over at the *Tilbury Hotel* before embarking on another leg of their world travels. When the Tilbury Docks were opened in 1886 great ships, that found difficulty in reaching the inner docks upriver in

London, came here instead. They were almost dwarfed by the 56 acres of dock entered through an open tidal basin of 18 acres. The Orient was the most important trading area for Tilbury in the early days. Since then the docks at Tilbury have been frequently enlarged to keep pace with the increasing size of shipping. About 1927 the largest vessels using Tilbury Docks were those of the P&O Steam Navigation Company, 633.6 feet long by 75.2 feet beam. It was inevitable that as passenger liners grew in size a passenger landing

44 (*top*)   Aerial view of Tilbury showing the Orient Line berths.

45 (*above left*)   The Central Dock at Tilbury, with lighters for goods and liners for passengers in the great days of the liners.

46 (*left*)   The Tilbury Hailing Station on the Thames collected information on incoming coal cargoes and telegraphed it to the East London docks up-river to help with berthing and unloading.

47 The Hospital at Tilbury provided by the Seamen's Hospital Society, seen here about 1920, was a much needed institution in a port which thousands of merchant seamen visited.

48 The Norwegian Seamen's Mission at Stanford-le-Hope, inland from Tilbury, was a sign of the presence of sailors of all nations.

49   The SS *Armadale* passing the *Tilbury Hotel* on its way down the Thames, *c.*1925. J.E. Caswell of Orient Road, Tilbury, published this postcard.

stage would be needed to allow the landing and embarkation of ocean-going passengers. From that time on the floating stage has seen bigger and bigger ships towering over the shore and rising deck upon deck above it.

Tilbury became an embarkation point for emigration to Australia. The London, Midland and Scottish Railway built a large terminal hall with customs facilities. After the war a famous incident was the docking of the *Empire Windrush* with its complement of hopeful West Indian immigrants taking the opposite route to the British folk who had gone to Australia. Later there was a period of decline, Tilbury Riverside station was closed, and the passenger train connection was replaced by a bus. Simpler passenger handling arrangements are now in force while the shipping hall is a revered monument to the past and a conservation project dear to enthusiasts. Tilbury's

fascination as a port in the days of the Cold War after 1945 lay partly in the arrival and departure of ships from behind the Iron Curtain. Vessels such as the *Michael Kalinin* sailed to and from Leningrad and gave inquisitive locals a small glimpse of what seemed like another world. Other Russian vessels also came up the Thames and occasionally a sailor would slip away from his ship seeking asylum in Britain. Rudolph Robert wrote in the 1960s that

> although Tilbury is at a disadvantage when compared with Constable Country (in picturesqueness) … there is a certain fascination in the flat countryside, in the winding Thames with its mud banks and white-winged gulls, in the forest of cranes and derricks. Best of all, perhaps, in the shipping – the cargo boats, the passenger liners, the tugs and the sailing barges, constantly coming and going.

FOUR

Villages of the Hidden East

ೞ೫౫ಎ

Little Thurrock

This parish is immediately adjacent to the town at Grays on the eastern side. It is narrow, from west to east, and is often thought of as part of Grays itself. The naming of the East Thurrock Road, which leads to the parish, is also misleading. William White, in his 1848 publication on Essex, describes it:

A village and parish, on the north bank of the Thames, one mile east of Grays Thurrock, and two miles N.W. of Tilbury Fort. It contains 301 souls, and about 1,400 acres of land, rising boldly from the marshes, and generally fertile and well cultivated ... It is now in three manors, called Little Thurrock, Tyrells Hall and Berewes, and belonging to the Bowlby, Jordan, Wheeler and other families. The church [Virgin Mary] is an

50   Rectory Road, Little Thurrock, with its modern houses in 1912.

51 On the way down to the docks in Little Thurrock is the appropriately named *Ship Inn*. The tower of Little Thurrock church is seen beyond.

ancient structure, with a nave and chancel of one pace. The rectory … is in the patronage and incumbency of the Revd E. Bowlby, who has a large and commodious residence. In this and adjacent parishes are some of those caverns in the chalk called Cunobelin's gold mines, and supposed to have been used as granaries by the ancient Britons, and as hiding holes by the Danes.

As well as the Revd Bowlby, White lists eight other significant professions: John Clark, maltster; Robert and Thomas Ingram, brick makers; Robert Ingram, farmer at Tyrells Hall; Edward Lees, victualler of the *Ship* public house; Samuel Smeeton, baker; James Travers, butcher; Abraham Turp, victualler at the *Bull* public house; and Thomas Winnett, a grocer.

Whitehall Lane Pit became a notable feature of the landscape and still houses various industrial concerns today. In the late 19th and early 20th centuries the parish became much more built up and even boasted its own shopping center, the Broadway. A First and Second World War memorial sits at a little crossroads on a high bank above the highway.

Chadwell St Mary

White calls this:

> A small scattered village, about two and a half miles E. of Grays Thurrock and S. of Orsett, [which] has in its parish 236 souls and 1,753 acres of land, extending southwards to the Thames and including part of Tilbury Fort. The soil is generally deep and heavy, and the lands rising above the marshes in this and neighbouring parishes, are distinguished by extensive chalk works, many of them of great antiquity, and forming large caverns, from 55 to 80 feet deep, though having only small openings at the top. The Revd J.P. Herringham is lord of the manor of Chadwell Hall, formerly held by the Bishop of London, and the Halton Cooke Velly, and other

52 The old 'Sleepers' farmhouse sits quietly at the crossroads in Chadwell St Mary in the mid-20th century.

53 The church of St Mary and the *Cross Keys* inn accompany the farmhouse at the main crossroads in Chadwell.

families. The small manor of Ingleby was held by a family of its own name, but it now belongs to the poor of Winchester, and that Bigging belongs to the Dean and Chapter of St Pauls. The Church [Virgin Mary] stands on the side of a hill, and has a nave and chancel of one pace, and a lofty stone tower containing two bells.

In 1848 Jane Ennever was the victualler at the *Cross Keys* inn, which stands at the crossroads opposite the church, its name suggesting that it was once the church hostel for pilgrims and travellers. Mrs Martha Jackson acted as a kind of postmistress at this time, receiving letters via Grays Thurrock and dispatching them. She may have delivered the letters around the village herself. Seven farmers are mentioned, so this was still the major economic activity of the

parish. The southern end of the parish became the site of the new extensive docks and town of Tilbury in the late 19th century, which outgrew its mother village.

Stanford-Le-Hope

White says of this place in 1842 that it

is a small village on a small rivulet [the Hassingbrook – a name that described the place in Doomsday book] about one and a half miles north of that portion of the Thames called The Hope; two miles S.E. of Horndon-on-the-Hill … A bridge crosses the rivulet on the site of the ancient stone-ford, which gave name to the village. The parish contains 336 inhabitants and 2,418 acres of land, extending southward to the Thames, and bounded on the west by Mucking, and on the east by Corringham; but

extended northward to Horndon and Lainden hills. J. Scratton is now lord of the manors, called Hassingbrook and Abbot's Hall, the former of which … was successively held by the Montchensy, Vere, Valence, Wettenhall and Featherston families. One of the latter built Hassingbrook Hall in the reign of James I. Abbot's Hall was given by Wm. de Semeles to Waltham Abbey, and after the dissolution,

---

54 (*left*)   The vision of a new life in Balstonia, Stanford-le-Hope was offered by Homesteads Ltd in 1908. The company offered homes in many other counties of England. The bungalow illustrated was typical and there are many examples of the original homes still to be seen in Stanford to this day, although the location is a little further from the station than indicated here.

55 (*above*)   An aerial view of Stanford in about 1930 shows a mix of Victorian and later housing and other buildings, with some modern shops standing out.

it passed to the Farr, Curson, Aleyn and other families. An estate called Calbourne, or Canvers, was formerly held by the Newenton, Henisey and Hallingworth families. Part of the parish belongs to several smaller proprietors, and the soil is fertile and well cultivated. The Church [St Margaret] is an ancient structure standing on rising ground and consisting of a nave with aisles, a chancel, and a tower. The interior has many monumental inscriptions, and had anciently a chantry endowed with lands which were granted at the dissolution to Wm. Golding … The Free School, held in part of the church was founded by Eliz. Davison, who in 1789 left her residuary property to four of her relations for their lives, and after the death of the survivor, churchwardens, and overseers of Stanford-le-Hope, for the support of a free school for poor children.

The postmaster in 1848 was Herbert Edward Massey; letters were dispatched at 3.30 p.m. and went via Romford. Two 'victuallers' are mentioned in 1848; David Beckwith at the *Cock*

56 Stanford-le-Hope's King Street shops at an early stage of development in about 1907.

57 (*top*)   The *Bull* at Corringham, a timeless feature of Corringham's old 'Churchtown' area, in the mid-20th century.

58 (*left*)   Wooden housing at Corringham and its two inhabitants at the beginning of the 20th century.

and Magpie and William Morley at the *King's Head*. Also mentioned in the directory are a shopkeeper, a builder and wheelwright, a blacksmith, a shoemaker and nine farmers. Thomas Radford is described as a surgeon, and William Wilson is given the title 'Chief constable'.

Since those days Stanford has acquired a railway station on the line between London and Southend and, in the 20th century, a considerable increase in housing, making it something of a commuter town. One notable development was that of Balstonia, about a mile north of the village, the centre of which by the church hill still retains quite a village atmosphere. There is a notable tomb in the churchyard known as Adam's Tomb, which has a kind of baldachino over the top of it. This was once incorporated in the actual wall of the church and is dated 1765. T.G. Key remembered that while working on the railway in the 1920s his 'gang' would buy a crate of Blyth and Squires 'Blue Label' beer, produced by that brewery in Stanford-le-Hope and costing the princely sum of one shilling and tuppence. The brewery was by the station, on the site where R. Boag Ltd later had their premises. Barley for this beer was prepared in the Maltings, located in Victoria Road.

Corringham

Corringham today has spread out across the fields towards Stanford-le-Hope. In 1890 the village consisted mainly of the attractive 'Churchtown', a small area at the heart of the settlement including the *Bull Inn*, about 350 years old but containing a gabled cross-wing about 200 years older still. At the top of the lane was a farmyard. Fortunately this scene has survived and the *Bull Inn* been modernised without losing its charm. From this little plot of peace one would have heard the children in the nearby parish school repeating their times-tables and other knowledge learnt by rote. *Kelly's Directory* in 1890 describes Corringham as

a village and parish, 14 miles south east from Brentwood and 2 east from Stanford-le-Hope station on the London, Tilbury and Southend railway. In the South Eastern division of the county (Electoral division), Barstable hundred, Orsett union and petty sessional division, Brentwood county court district, and in the rural deanery of Orsett, archdeaconry of Essex and diocese of St Albans. The church of St Mary the Virgin is a small building of flint and stone in the Early English style, consisting of church, nave, north aisle with chantry, north porch and a massive tower with pyramidal roof, containing three bells, respectively dated 1580, 1617 and 1629; it was originally a Norman church, but of this only the tower remains; the nave is separated from aisle by an arcade of two bays; a fine old oak-screen still exists in the chantry, which is presumably that founded by William de Baud in 1328 and still retains a little old glass; there is a trefoil headed piscina in the south wall of the chancel, and a stoup in the south porch; there are brasses to Richard de Beltoun, a former rector, circa 1340, with a half-length effigy; to Alice Gravye, ob.1453; Thomas Attlee, ob.1464, and Margaret his wife; and to Robert Draper, also a former incumbent, ob.1595, this brass being inserted in an ancient stone inscribed 'Abele: baud: gist: ici: diev: de: sa: alme: eit: merci:'. There is also the figure of a female *c.*1460, much worn … the entire structure except the tower was restored in 1833-4 by … Sir G. Gilbert Scott, at the chief cost of the rector: the tower was restored in 1864, and the north aisle in 1875 … The soil [of the parish] is mixed; subsoil, gravel and clay. The chief crops are wheat, barley, beans, peas and clover. The area is 3,415 acres of land, with much marsh and 747 of water, reaching to the Thames … the population in 1871 was 273.

Included in the parish commercial list are the Rushbrook Brothers, brickmakers, Tilbury brickfields carrying on the tradition of Daniel Defoe. As well as several farmers, Israel Alston, baker and shopkeeper, John James Crussell, shoemaker, Mrs Mary Philpot, beer retailer, James Ransom, blacksmith, and Thomas Wright, carpenter, are important members of the community. William Such was landlord at the *Bull Inn*.

After the Conquest, Corringham manor was split into three smaller manors: Corringham, Old Hall and Coggers. The Baud family of Corringham manor, who were in charge from 1174-1550, were well connected. Simon de Baud was killed in 1174 while on a Crusade. A further member of the family lost his life in Gallicia in 1189 fighting the Saracens. Sir William Baud was connected with a strange custom which took place in St Paul's Cathedral from 1272 until Queen Elizabeth's reign. In exchange for 22 acres of a cathedral manor of West Lee, Sir William had to grant St Paul's 'yearly and forever, on the feast of the conversion of St Paul, in winter, a good doe, seasonable and sweet, and in summer, on the feast of the commemoration of the saint, a good buck to be offered on the high altar, the same to be spent among the canons-resident'. Specific instructions were laid out concerning how this ceremony was to be conducted, the whole thing apparently a relic of rituals from pagan times.

Mucking

As has been pointed out on several occasions, Mucking is unfortunate in that it is bisected by a railway, has been scarred by a gravel pit and has been engulfed by boatloads of refuse which have been brought here along the Thames since

the marshlands were selected as a suitable site for this activity. The name itself is suggestive to modern ears. But obscured by these problems are wonderful treasures, either conferred by nature, or laid down in the parish by its early inhabitants. From 1965 Mucking was the site for an excavation that produced evidence of successive eras of ancient inhabitation and, very specially, a magnificent Saxon community that has advanced our knowledge of these ancient peoples. From the natural history point of view there are still footpaths across the landscape that bring home the loneliness and beauty of Mucking's marshes and recall the solitary lives spent in isolated farmsteads in previous centuries.

On the the main road from Stanford to Grays still stands a Georgian building formerly called by various names, including St Clere's Hall and New Jenkins among others. Jenkins appears to derive from a 16th-century individual mentioned in a document granting properties to a Ralph Thoroughgood. The mansion was later occupied by James Adams, whose ornate and unusual tomb can be seen at Stanford-le-Hope. The church of St John the Baptist sits under a canopy of trees and is now a private residence. In front, on the roadside, is the old village school. Other buildings of interest are Walton's Hall, perpetuating the name of the other post-Conquest manor, Gobions, Blue House Farm, which has a combined barn and dovecote, access to the latter being by a ladder from inside the granary and Old Jenkins. Nearer the Thames area and the refuse landfill project is a survivor of the old village known as Surridge's Farm or Crown Inn (a previous transformation).

An attempt in the 20th century to bury the old name of the parish resulted in a shopping

development and some housing in the fields, well away from the main village, named Linford.

East and West Tilbury

East Tilbury is described by White in 1848 as

> an ancient village on the north bank of the Thames, at the east end of Gravesend Reach, and at the south end of that broad bend of the river, commonly called The Hope; about two and a half miles E. by N. of Tilbury Fort … Its parish contains 311 inhabitants, and 2031 acres of land and includes part of New Kingsford, about a mile from the church. The Roman road called Higham causeway, of which some trace yet remains between Rochester and Higham, points in the direction of the ancient ferry of East Tilbury, which is believed to have been the place where the Emperor Claudius crossed the Thames in pursuit of the Britons, as related by Dion Cassius. The land is now nearly all freehold

59 (*top*) These cottages at East Tilbury, close to the road, exhibit features of the older dwellings on the edge of the marshland.

60 (*above*) East Tilbury Rectory at the end of the 19th century, impressive grandeur in a village setting.

61 (*left*)   Drawing of a typical drover on the Tilbury marshes, 1900s.

62 (*opposite*)   Tilbury Fort in the late 18th century.

and William Cotton, one of the Governors of the Bank of England, is the principal owner. It is in five manors or estates, viz. East Tilbury, St Clere's, Gobions, Gossaline and Southall. The latter is vested in trust for the repairs of Rochester Bridge. Another estate here was purchased in 1729 for the endowment of Limehouse rectory. The church (St Katharine) is an ancient structure consisting of a nave, north aisle and chancel. Its tower which stood at the south-west angle, was beaten down by the Dutch, in the reign of Charles II.

In 1848, Archibald Thomas was victualler at the *Ship* tavern, William Creed was similarly at the *World's End*, Tilbury Ferry and Charles Bond was described as a shopkeeper. East Tilbury was the site of a Romano-British settlement, the remains now being concealed on the foreshore between the high and low water levels. Even today the road dips down, forming what was once a path to the ferry. Also here, cutting off the view of the Thames, is Coalhouse Fort, which has grown from the blockhouse set down on the shore in Henry VIII's time to guard this reach of the river. East Tilbury was reputedly the site of St Chad's mission to convert the

people of Essex. He became Bishop of York in AD 666 and an old legend places his stone coffin in the churchyard. There are also the remains of earthworks inland, and the old sea wall constructed by the Danes on the shore could be seen until the 19th century.

West Tilbury

White records this as

a small village at the head of a small creek of the Thames, nearly two miles W. of East Tilbury. It has in its parish 516 souls and 1,687 acres of land, including Tilbury Fort, which rears its frowning battlements on the north bank of the Thames, opposite Gravesend, to which it has a busy ferry. Queen Elizabeth established her army here in 1588, when the kingdom was threatened by the Spanish Armada; traces of the encampment may be seen near the fort. The Queen came here and delivered to the army a long patriotic address, in which she said, 'My loving people, We have been persuaded by some that are careful of our safety, to take heed how we commit ourselves to armed multitudes, for fear of treachery; but I assure you, that I do not live to distrust my loving and faithful people; let tyrants fear.'

Tilbury Fort is partly in the parish of Chadwell St Mary. West Tilbury is said to have had a considerable town in the seventh century, called Tillaburgh, where St Chad, bishop of the East Saxons, built a church when spreading the English religion in this county. A mineral spring was discovered in the parish in 1727, about 12 feet above the surface of a small eminence, rising above the marshes. The soil is freehold and belongs to various owners.

The church (St James) is pleasantly situated on rising ground, from which there is an extensive prospect over the estuary of the Thames. Formerly it had a lofty stone tower, which fell down many years ago, when a wooden framed tower and spire were built on its site. The body of the church was also rebuilt, and now consists of a nave, chancel and porch. A gravestone in the shape of a coffin and ornamented with crosses, forms the sill of one of the windows, but was formerly in the north aisle of the original church. A chapel anciently stood on the site of the Fort, dedicated to St Mary Magdalene, and founded in the time of St Thomas à Becket. It was called West Lee Chapel, and is supposed to have been founded by one of the Tilbury family. Presumably this chapel was built for pilgrims who crossed the river here on their way to Canterbury.

Most of the locals at the time of this account in 1848 were engaged in farming. Five farmers are listed in the directory. One of these is also a coal merchant, coal being landed from the river at nearby East Tilbury. In the village, as well as the *King's Head* public house run by Edward Travis, who was also a builder, there was another beer seller called James Waylett, Thomas Wilson, a police officer, John Ranson, a blacksmith, Joseph James, a corn miller, Richard Grover, a grocer, William Harris, a baker, and J. Gladwin, a shoemaker. The church today is

63   A smuggler's signal lantern. The visible top
light meant the coast was clear. The bottom two
lights spelt danger and the message: do not land
your cargoes tonight.

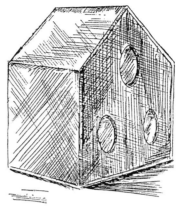

64   The tower of St Michael's, Fobbing, a beacon for shipping and a target for the Dutch fleet which
sailed up the Thames in 1667. It used to overlook the tiny harbour that existed at the bottom of the hill.
The *Ship Inn*'s publican catered for the bargemen and workers from a local brickfield.

65   The picturesque appearance of the *White Lion* derives partly from its position on Lion Hill just below the main village. Built originally in the 15th century, the inn celebrated Oak-Apple Day, 29 May, with great festivity.

a private residence but the *King's Head* is still open for business.

Fobbing

Fobbing stands on a pinnacle above the wide marshes, seemingly detached from the modern world, and has an almost mythic air about it, seeming to echo with tales from a long distant past. This is probably on account of the number of local people involved in the Peasants' Revolt.

It is a pity that a link with former times was severed when the wharf at the bottom end of Wharf Lane was closed in 1953. From the churchyard above the old creek one can look out over the extensive marshland and imagine the scene when boats tacked up the creek with all its twists and turns. Local knowledge was certainly valuable in the smuggling days, when cargoes of contraband were quietly offloaded in the creek. Tales of those days involve the numerous cellars that have existed under houses and other buildings in the village.

When the Dutch fleet sailed up the Thames a lookout on the church tower saw the flash of a cannon discharged in his direction. It missed the tower, but not by much, as the ball lodged in the wooden part of the porch. The village of Fobbing provided a ship for the Royal Navy in 1629 and in the same year four bells were placed in the tower. St Michael's church has a complete list of its clergy since 1325 when Robert de Tonge was the incumbent. One name stands out: John Hopton was chaplain and confessor to Mary Tudor when she was a princess. He went on to become Bishop of Norwich.

The historian of London, Stow, said that Jack Cade's rebellion began in the village of Fobbing and that the mob broke into a nearby priory and 'drank up three tuns of wine, and devoured all the victuals'. In 1842 the parish contained 428 inhabitants, and 2,632 acres, give or take a little, but this land was 'mostly in low marshes, extending to the Thames and intersected and nearly encompassed by several creeks of that river, one of which called East or Hole Haven flows on the western end of Canvey Island and runs four miles inland to Pitsea.' By 1890 what White calls 'an out-port of London' had been created on the Thames and the London, Tilbury and Southend railway had built a branch line to it running off the passenger line at Stanford-le-Hope. This was being used for the transport of cattle, and there was a special dock for unloading these animals from the small vessels. There was even a public house at Thames Haven called the *Dock House*, the licensee being George Ockendon.

In 1890 'the soil is upland, mixed; marsh lands, heavy; subsoil, various'. The main crops at the time were wheat, barley, oats, beans, peas, clover and tares. The population had hardly changed from 1842.

FIVE

Northward along the Heights

South Ockendon

St Nicholas church is an ancient structure with a round embattled tower, one of a select number in Essex and even in Britain. At one time the tower was crowned by a wooden spire but this was destroyed by lightning in 1638. The main door is surrounded by a fine Norman arch of an excellent design incorporating most of the distinctive features of Norman decoration: chevron billet, pellet and dog tooth. Inside the church there are various memorials of the former knightly families of Bruyn and Saltonstall. Former manors were Bruyns and Groves. The manor of Bruyns, with the estate of South

66   Outside the centre of the village Ockendon became open and rural, as the view of the Chase in the first decade of the 20th century confirms.

Ockendon Hall, which amounted to 666 acres, once belonged to the executors of the late John Cliff and was offered for sale in 1847, realising the sum of £24,620. It was then occupied by Mr T.B. Sturgeon, who was a noted breeder of merino sheep and raiser of livestock for export. This family continued to farm in South Ockendon into the 20th century and their name appeared on milk bottles delivered in the village before the Second World War.

In 1848 South Ockendon was 'a large village, partly round the margins of a green … Its parish has generally a flat surface and contains 968 souls and 2,872 acres of land.' South Ockendon

67 The moat, bridge and gateway to the vanished South Ockendon Hall in 1930. This was once the noble residence of the Bruyn family. The top of the gatehouse consists of 17th-century bricks which rest on squared-up medieval blocks of Reigate Stone.

supported a good number of tradesmen at this time, suggesting it was a prosperous place. David Beard was the baker and the miller was Thomas Bennett Sturgeon, who was also the farmer and breeder at The Hall. Two public houses are mentioned and Samuel Sweeting, the victualler at the *Red Lion*, also carried on the trade of joiner. At the *Plough* public house, Charles and Isaac Willey were the licensees. There was also a tinner and brazier (Thomas Collis), a tailor and draper (Nicholas Birch), a builder and carpenter (Abraham Davey), and a bricklayer and blacksmith (William Pain). It sounds as though quite a bit of house building was going on at this time. Horses and their needs were catered for by William Drayton and Edward Fisk, who were farriers, and Josiah Kirkham, who was a saddler, and there was a wheelwright, William Elsdon. Three other important people were William Horncastle, the schoolmaster, Robert Binks Jordison, surgeon and registrar and, to keep everyone in order, Charles Everett, the policeman.

The South Ockendon Methodist church had been erected in 1847. Before this date, the Wesleyans had met in the large kitchen of a Mr Smith, at 'The Mount' in the High Street, now called South Road. When the railway to the village was opened, the preachers would come by train on Sunday morning and stay for the day, addressing the Sunday School in the afternoon.

68 (*below*)   South Ockendon's peaceful heart in about 1900. Brwick cottages and some Essex vernacular timber houses face the surprisingly well advertised Ockendon Stores of Alfred Kimber, which suggests a prosperous village at this time.

69 (*top right*)   North Road, South Ockendon in the 1920s, with buildings of different ages forming a ribbon development where the highway northwards leaves the built-up village for the open fields. An inconspicuous notice high up on the wall on the left announces the business of James Edward Vaughan, Dairyman. This faces an almost suburban row of other shops with which the village was beginning to be well served.

70 (*below right*)   South Hill climbs up to 1930s Horndon village, passing thatched houses and other structures before the days of frequent motor traffic. The famous *Bell Inn*, going back centuries, can be seen on the hill's summit.

The Church of St Peter and Paul is tucked away among its pollarded lime trees amidst the weathered monuments of village notables like the 18th-century Westwoods, wealthy farmers, and the Tyrells, Victorian shopkeepers. Horndon Woolmarket, a timber-framed building with an upper chamber once used as a manor court, was put up about 1525 by the Shaa (pronounced Shaw) family. The open ground-floor bays were used as a market for the sale of woollen cloth, Horndon being the centre for textile operations and having a fulling mill on the Hassenbrook stream at the foot of the hill. Saffron flowers for dyeing cloth were grown in local fields and one of the parish farms is still called Saffron Gardens.

Bulphan

Three miles north-west of Horndon, this peaceful village had 254 inhabitants and 1,651 acres of land in 1848. The church of the Virgin Mary is a small ancient structure sited at the heart of the village. Until the Dissolution the manor was held by Barking Abbey. By 1881 the population had increased to just 284.

Much of this land is known as Bulphan Fen and descends westwards to a small stream. Looking across the landscape from the edge of the village the flat fields disappear into the distance, apparently endless, the great attraction being the ever-changing panorama of the skies. This landscape is dotted with farms, often seemingly

Horndon-on-the-Hill

Horndon has a number of historic buildings, including a newsagent's in a 15th-century building, originally part of a timber-framed 'hall house', Grices, a tall gabled house with a Tudor interior including a brick cellar of *c.* 1550, and the Old House, with excellent Tudor chimney stacks, at one time Horndon's Parsonage. It is reputed that General Fairfax's Parliamentary forces stayed at Grices en route to the Colchester siege in June 1648. In Edward the Confessor's time, a mint located in the village briefly issued silver pennies.

72 Walking in the middle of the road between the *Swan* pub (right) and post office (left) in 1930s Horndon.

73 Nearer the heart of the village and church is the Bulphan schoolhouse, seen about 1910.

placed in the middle of nowhere. A document of 1836 describes 'Bulvan' (as it was then written) as 'south from Dunton and extends west to the Brook which in its course to Purfleet by the reflux of this tide considerably overflowed the country producing the marsh lands of Orsett and Bulphan fens.'

There is a tradition that at high tide boats could once sail up this stream as far as Orsett Hall. E.H. Rowley, who had an encyclopaedic knowledge of farmers and farmlands of the district, said, 'the Flete river eventually became the Mardyke. The only boat I ever heard of was at Stifford when I was a boy. Mr Fred Wagstaff,

74   On the Thurrock border, about 228 feet above sea level, is the former *Red Cow* (right) at Dry Street, seen in about 1908. This was used as an off-licence, but in 1933 became a post office with an outside post box. It has since been demolished.

Rowley possessed an old farming account book in which there were several entries relating to floods in the 18th century. Of Bulphan fen, on 21 June 1766, the writer states, 'very large flood, the boat went to the Harrow and later on lent my boat to William Stevens to fetch his daughter Bet from the Ockendon Fen gate'.

In the old days the locals spoke of the 'fan' rather than the fen. The rights of grazing on Bulphan Fen were not regulated by Parliamentary Act, but managed by a committee elected by the local farmers until the Second World War, when the County Agricultural Committee turned over the fen to corn growing, although some grazing was still allowed. An enquiry at the beginning of the 1960s ended in the holders of grazing rights being compensated and the fen being let to five tenants for cultivation.

Langdon Hills

It is claimed that the interest in Langdon Hills is mainly scenic and not historical or archaeological. The author most quoted on this point is Arthur Young, who wrote in his 'Southern tour' in the 18th century:

> One of the most astonishing [sights] to be beheld breaks out almost at once upon one of the dark lanes. Such a prodigious valley, everywhere painted with the finest verdure and intersected with numerous hedges and woods, appears beneath you, that it is past description; the Thames winding through it, full of ships and bounded by the hills of Kent ... I beg you will go and view this enchanting scene, though a journey of forty miles be necessary for it. I never beheld anything like it in the west of England, that region of landscapes!

who lived at Coppid Hall, had a small boat with a sail. When the stream was full and the wind right it sailed up towards Bulphan, but as there was no room to tack he had to punt back.'

The remaining woods are still attractive.

In recent years a Country Park has been created to explain man's effect on the

75   On the north boundary of Thurrock is Bulphan's Fen Lane, not all that changed today from this view in the mid-20th century, with the rolling acres of farmland beyond.

environment, and the history which the area is supposed to have! A number of artefacts from the prehistoric era have surfaced. There are two churches, a modern building on the summit and the partly 16th-century All Saints church halfway down the Western hill, which has unusual shape like a capital L, the foot forming the north chapel. Thomas Richards has a floor slab memorial which recalls 'a man who in these unhappy times when tyranny had usurpt the throne and schism too farre prevailed in this pulpit, so justly steered twixt each extream.' Thomas died in 1669 and his epitaph is redolent of the troubled days of the Commonwealth, when brother fought brother. Because of the time in which it was built, the church contains special features such

as box pews, gallery and three-decker pulpits, but was neglected in the 20th century.

White's description of 1848 runs,

Langdon Hills, a scattered village and parish on a lofty Eminence … has 288 inhabitants and 1,775 acres of land. The hill on which this parish stands is about a mile in length and breadth … From the north the ascent of the hill is gradual, but its other sides rise abruptly. Pleasure parties from the metropolis and other places often assemble round a large tree on the highest point, to enjoy the extensive and delightful view, in which is seen the broad bosom of the Thames for a distance of nearly forty miles, thickly studded with steam and sailing vessels; and a wide range of country in this county and Kent.

Six

Westward Prospects

North and South Stifford

The industrialisation of Thurrock has created a contrast between North and South Stifford. Glyn Morgan notes, 'It is easy to wax romantic over North Stifford', and goes on to point out the charm inherent in the grouping of old cottages, many of which are thatched. It has been traditional in the village for good craftsmen to be employed in renewing the thatch and other parts of these cottages and maintain the harmony which the original builders conferred on the surroundings through their effortless artistry and craftsmanship. The church of the Virgin Mary is an old building of flint and stone set down in its own 'God's acre'. Coppid Hall at the east end of the village is a Queen Anne-style building of 1756. The White House is a large residence nearby and Palin, a 19th-century compiler or local histories, records that Stifford Hall was sited to the south of it. From the time of Elizabeth I to that of Queen Anne the Lathom family lived here. Later it was the home of William Palmer, who founded the famous Thurrock school, and a neighbouring wood retained the name Palmer's Shaw. A cottage with an 18th-century chimney stack was once the *Oaks* inn; in the church

registers of 1721 it is noted that the Vestry ceased their efforts and adjourned to the *Oaks*.

The old road from the north over Stifford bridge was a pilgrims' way. At this west end of the village the pilgrim route to St Clement's forks right over the hill, and the road into the village climbs up to the present-day *Dog and Partridge*. Stifford heath, west of this, later the site of the Ardale homes, was in feudal times the meeting place for the annual court leet, or view of frank-pledge. The lord of the manor attended with the farmers of the village, the freemen, to ensure that all were working together to keep the peace, and any offences against the public good were penalised. Ford Place, north of the bridge, was once an important house, the seat of the Silverlocks. This house had been rebuilt in 1665. Nearer the church, in the centre of the village, a quaint cottage sits at the top of a lane along which pilgrims once came, crossing a minor ford to join the others before crossing the Thames at West Thurrock; this is perhaps the older route which may have dated back to prehistoric times. North Stifford sits on a shelf above the Mardyke, now only a small stream but in Roman times apparently a significant river that

76 (*right*) Thatched cottages, some with outside chimney breasts, near the church in the old-world part of North Stifford in the 1940s. Through the fields on either side once ran the pilgrim track on its way to the Thames below.

77 (*below right*) Cottages in Stifford in the 1920s were more workaday and fewer of the modern amenities were available.

boats could navigate upstream as far as Bulphan. A bronze sword and dagger and Samian ware (the attractive orange-coloured pottery) left behind by the Romans have been found in the bed of the stream. The church is of different periods: the north wall of the nave dates from the 12th century; in the 13th century the south chapel was added to the chancel, and about 1260-70 both the south aisle and the south arcade of the nave were built. The west tower may also date from this time.

Modern street names on the Stifford Clays estate recall the past. Fletthall was the second part of Stifford Manor when it was divided; Sir John Clays was one of the early possessors of this manor, and later came Anthony Bradshawe, John Durninge and Kenwrick Grantham. Jasper Kingsman, who was High Sheriff of Essex, is remembered in Kingsman Drive. Palins Way and Simmons Place owe their names to rectors of more modern times. Lords of the manor of Stifford were Henry De Crammavill (1269), the Ardalles, Sir Thomas Gourney (1620) and the Broderers' Company (1631 onwards). Lessors of this manor were William Palmer (1669) and Dr Hogarth, who was also rector 1821-34.

South Stifford, a narrow continuation of the parish southward to the Thames, contains part of the old London road and the 19th-century ribbon development between Grays and West Thurrock consisting mainly of working-class cottages. In contrast to the village, it bears the scars of an industrialised landscape and the remains of open pits.

West Thurrock

In 1848 White describes this place as a 'long, straggling village, extending more than a Mile along the road and the marshes on the north

78 (*above*) West Thurrock schools in about 1912.

79 (*opposite*) Teece's shop formed part of St James Terrace, West Thurrock in the first decade of the 20th century. This east-west road north of the Thames shore had developed gradually as the area became industrialised.

side of the Thames, opposite Greenhithe pier, and between Grays Thurrock and Purfleet'. At the time Purfleet, described as a hamlet, was part of this parish, which contained 2,863 acres of land and had 1,032 inhabitants in 1841. Only 328 were in West Thurrock. White says, 'about 400 of the inhabitants are employed in the extensive lime and chalk pits, worked by W.H. Whitbread, the lord of the manor and owner of most of the parish. W.D. Cooper and several smaller owners have estates in the parish.' A later commentator, E.H. Rowley, remembered

the Curtis family farming at West Thurrock and being celebrated for cattle breeding, so in the 19th century the parish economy was still balanced between agriculture and industry. The beginning of the century had seen the Napoleonic Wars, and English farmers and growers became rich supplying food and forage to the military and others while prices rose.

White points out that

West Hall, the old manor house, was formerly named Le Vineyard, from vines having been cultivated here in ancient times. It has latterly been called High House, from its situation on the side of a lofty hill, commanding a delightful prospect over the marshes and the river Thames … the church (St Clement) is a very ancient stone building with a massive tower containing three bells. It stands at the east end of the village, near the river bank.

When the riverside became industrialised the church was gradually dwarfed by factory buildings.

Pilgrims of the Middle Ages prayed and sought shelter here before crossing the Thames.

Pilgrims

A leaden badge recovered in April 1979 from a bank of the river Mardyke at Stifford provides a tantalising clue to a whole world of pilgrimage lasting around 300 years, about which very little is known. The rectangular plaque of 35 x 35 mm. would originally have had a stitching loop at each corner so that it could be fastened to clothes or to a hat. Depicted on the badge are half-length figures of St Peter and St Paul around which is inscribed 'Signa Apostolorum Petr et Pavli' (the signs of the apostles Peter and Paul). St Peter, on the right, holds his traditional attributes, a key and a long cross, symbolising his position as prince of the church and of the apostles. St Paul's upturned sword is the instrument and symbol of his martyrdom. St Peter is given curly hair and

80 Edwardian adults and children out for a walk on the promenade at Botany Terrace, where one house has been converted into a tearoom and shop.

beard, but the faces of both are similar to those that appear from the end of the 11th century on papal seals or bulls. This pilgrim sign from Rome was also discovered in an incomplete version on the Thames foreshore at Queenhithe in London in 1978. Others have been found in Rome, Lyons, Paris, Hamburg, Holbaek (Denmark), Bergen and Halsingborg, the last two datable to between about 1250 and 1300 by other known evidence. The pilgrim who lost his badge possibly crossing a rather turbulent Mardyke would have travelled between these dates. The latter was a very special holy year of jubilee when extra indulgences were offered to those visiting the Rome basilicas and the pilgrim involved would have found himself amid 200,000 others at any time during that year.

The evidence for particular named or identified 'pilgrim ways' cannot be traced back with any sureness more than a few centuries, but the finding of the badge gives credence to local people such as Palin, who

retained their belief in the local pilgrim routes without any ancient place-names in Thurrock to substantiate their theories. One such is that of Pilgrims Hatch, near Brentwood, where the remains of a medieval chapel dedicated to St Thomas are still to be seen in the town. As early as 1483 documents refer to 'Pylgremes hacch' and parish registers of 1539 and 1540 also mention

81 Crowds packed the beach at peak holiday weekends.

it. Pilgrims may not have always used the direct route, switching from one to the other of the roads available at the time to avoid dangerous woodland, where robbers and outlaws might be lurking. Hazardous marshes also posed a possible problem. St Clements, West Thurrock, must have been a ferry or crossing place, the popularity of which meant that pilgrims could travel in a fairly large party, the safest way when even locals were hostile. There were other possible crossings of the lower Thames which could be used but they were not so convenient on the Kent side.

Purfleet
Although part of West Thurrock, Purfleet is described by White in 1848 as having 704

inhabitants, but the figure included 199 persons in the barracks and

> 172 labourers in barns etc., so that the stationary population of the parish (of West Thurrock) is only about 700 souls ... Purfleet is a village and military station ... at the mouth of a rivulet, and at the west end of West Thurrock ... sometimes called a township ... and has a pleasure fair on the 13th of June. Near it are the extensive lime and chalk pits of W.H. Whitbread, the lord of the manor. The harbour is often full of shipping business and animation; and joining it is a large government powder magazine, consisting of five detached bomb-proof and well-protected store-houses, barracks for a company of artillery, a store keeper's mansion, and a good quay. The magazine was built in 1781, and has room for the safe keeping of 60,000 barrels of gunpowder. The village is on rising ground, and in the vicinity numerous romantic scenes are formed by the high projecting chalk rocks, interspersed with deep and extensive caverns. Of these chalk hills, and those on the Kentish side of the Thames, the lofty Beacon and Cliff which overlooks the village commands an extensive prospect ... Many thousand tons of lime are burnt annually and sent to London and other places; and from the kilns, railways are extended to the quarries, as well as to the shipping. The chalk cliffs are covered by several feet of surface loam, and from the magnitude of the excavations, appear to have been worked several centuries.

The directory mentions that in 1848 steam vessels to London and Gravesend, five times a day, could

82 Avenue North Buildings, at the top of the hill in Purfleet in about 1903, would be known only to locals and visitors who ventured further afield from the main attractions nearer the Thames.

83 Railway Terrace at Purfleet, seen before the First World War, is more recent than much of the other housing in the village. It contains C.H. Digby's shop, providing tobacco products, haberdashery, stationery, general stores and, of course, the ubiquitous supply of teas.

84 The railway's arrival in Purfleet in the mid-19th century turned the village into a tourist destination which was served by refreshment houses such as Cox and Palmer's Tea Garden, seen here about 1908.

be hailed by a boat from Purfleet, and that the post office was located at Peter Edwards' Barrack yard, and letters went via Romford daily. As well as the *Purfleet Hotel*, now the *Royal*, there were three other Inns: the *Fox and Goose*, the *Old Ship* and the *Rising Sun* as well as a beerhouse.

In 1768 the Essex historian Morant wrote, 'Near Purfleet, among the hills, are very Great chalk pits and lime works which bring

considerable profit to the Bricklayers' Company that took a lease of them from Caleb Grantham.' Caleb, like his father, worked for the East India Company, rising to the rank of captain, afterwards quitting the sea to become a director of London Assurance from 1744-56 and, whilst in Thurrock, he lived at High House. In 1906 the Revd W.J. Hayes, investigating a vault in St Clement's church, found a number of coffins. One, inscribed

85 (*left*) Purfleet Crossing. The photographer has captured this middle-class outing by horse carriage to sample the delights of Purfleet's attractions in the 1890s. The signal box behind awaits the next train with more working-class trippers.

86 (*top*) The Training Ship *Cornwall* was moored off Purfleet to provide a nautical and disciplinary regime for the education of boys in need of care. Seen here in the 1890s, the vessel was removed to Gravesend in 1928. After damage by enemy action in 1940 she was broken up in 1948. However, her teak timbers were found to be in such good condition that they were used in the rebuilding of the Law Courts in London.

with the name of Nathaniel Grantham, Caleb's father, and dated 1723, contained a liquid. When the lead cover was rolled back, the coffin revealed the face of Nathaniel, well preserved as he had been pickled in rum, fittingly enough for an ex-naval commander.

By the 19th century the Purfleet chalk works and half the village belonged to the Whitbread family, but quite a bit of the river frontage was

in different hands. Over the centuries the sea wall, such as it was, broke down and flooded the marsh land all around Purfleet, ruining crops and adversely affecting cattle. It even affected passage of larger ships to London. The owners of the inundated land seemed powerless to prevent the flooding owing to the cost of any operations, so, in the early 18th century, the government sent for skilful Dutch embanker

87 (*above*)   Looking down Aveley High Street about 1906. A long fence leads down to the *Crown and Anchor* inn. The road surface could certainly do with some improvement.

88 (*opposite, top*)   Houses from several periods lined the High Street at Aveley in about 1913. Newer slate roofs contrast with tiled ones of uncertain vintage. Next to brick buildings there are wooden structures faced with plaster and the odd gas lamp here and there.

89 (*opposite, below*)   Outside the Lodge, Aveley about 1903, its attractive iron gates leading to parkland. A gap in the wooden fence is wide enough to allow a youngster into the park.

Cornelius Vandenanker and his team to rebuild the wall completely and redeem the marshes. They did such a good job they were given the land redeemed from the river as their reward, which they later sold. And so the land passed into other hands.

The Whitbreads owned the manor of West Thurrock from 1777 to 1920 and for 140 years more or less they were able to control the development of their portion of the parish and particularly the village of Purfleet. The estate was bought out of profits made from Samuel Whitbread's London brewery. The family possessed 342 acres in Purfleet including 1,300 feet of river frontage as well as a jetty. The Revd

90 This public house on the Purfleet Road, Aveley provides benches outside for these youngsters. The beer is supplied by Fielder's Brewery in Brentwood. A hay cart rumbles down the lane in the distance.

J. Hayes eventually purchased Lot 40 after Samuel Whitbread Jnr decided to sell the whole estate, and a temporary church was built close to the parsonage which had been built from materials taken from old Purfleet House, which was cut in two to enable this to be done.

In 1854 the railway from London came to Purfleet and thousands of people decided that the village was an interesting place for a day out, possibly attracted by illustrated accounts of the great white cliffs through which the railway had been cut. The quarry had been closed down by 1850 and turned into pleasure gardens. This had led to a fall in population by a third between 1841 and 1851. But now Purfleet became a holiday resort and other amusements soon sprang up. Tea gardens opened beside the village green

and before terraced houses previously occupied by labourers. Boatmen offered trips across the river to *Long Reach* tavern, or to see the training ship *Cornwall* moored off Purfleet. A favourite stroll was up to the top of Beacon Hill where a good view could be obtained of the Botany Gardens and the Thames. Where the chalk had been stripped away over the years there remained cliffs almost 100 feet high and even some detached islands. But the gardens were the real delight. Whitbread's gardeners looked after the Botany and no charge was levied to enter them. Thousands returned home by train refreshed after outings to this popular playground of the masses, Thursdays and Saturdays being the most popular days for a visit. By 1909, the last year of the famous Purfleet fair held on 13 June, the popularity of the resort was declining. In the words of a newspaper of the time, there was a 'regular battle' that year after one of the showmen threatened a police officer with an axe. In fact the riverside's frontage was now being occupied by industrial concerns again, and even the quarry had been reopened at the turn of the century.

Aveley

Aveley's name probably derives from the 'leah' or meadow of Aelfgyth, believed to have been a lady. In Domesday Book it is spelt Aluithelea. It was subsequently divided into four manors: Aveley, Belhouse, Bumpstead and Bretts, the names of which survive locally. The original village can be seen to have been built on a Saxon model: the cottages, inns, buttermarket and early shops stood close around the church. The oldest part of the church is the group of Norman pillars and semi-circular arches of the south arcade, built about 1160. The north arcade is early 13th century and the chancel and its adjacent chapel are also from that century, as is the lower part of the western tower. In 1848 White describes the church of St Michael as an 'ancient structure, with a nave and aisles, a chancel, and a square tower of flint and stone, containing five bells, and crowned with a small wooden spire, erected in lieu of a lofty one that was blown down in 1703 (the year of the great storm)'.

91 The South Drawing Room at Belhus illustrated in the Sale Catalogue of the contents which were dispersed in 1923.

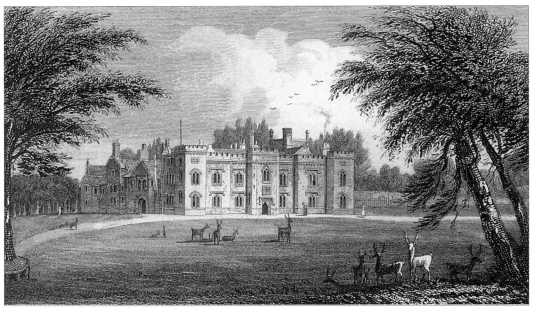

92 (*top*)   Belhus Mansion in the 18th century.

93 (*above*)   The great fireplace and overmantel from Belhus preserved in the Thurrock Museum at Grays.

He describes Aveley as

a long pleasant village, on a bold acclivity … Its parish contains 2,852 acres including 162 acres of wood; and had 849 inhabitants in 1841, but 113 of them were labourers, only temporarily resident, when the census was taken. Aveley had anciently a market, and has still a fair on Whit Monday … but a great part of the parish belongs to other proprietors, the largest of whom is Sir Thomas Barrett Lennard, bart who has a handsome seat here called Belhus from the knightly family of Belhus, who were seated here in the reigns of King John and Henry III. The present large and stately mansion was built here in the reign of Henry VII, but has since been considerably enlarged and beautified, and is surrounded by an extensive park, containing some fine deer, and an abundance of large forest trees. It is a noble specimen of the Tudor style of architecture.

Although the deer have gone, some of the trees have survived in the open spaces on the Belhus housing estate, built after the Second World War, after Belhus mansion had been demolished and the noble estate dispersed.

SEVEN

Industrial Revolutions

CB EO

Farming is the most ancient skill to have survived as the occupation of the major part of the working population into modern times. Many advances and developments in agriculture were developed in Essex or pioneered on local farms. One of the more famous enterprises was the Belhus estate, and a great number of family farms, including those cultivated by families like the Watts, who came down from Scotland, introduced significant improvements and new crops to the land. Just to the north of Thurrock is Stubbers, where the tomato and the Jerusalem artichoke were imported and grown in England for the first time.

At one time each village was reliant on access to a working mill to produce the flour to make the bread from the wheat grown in its own fields. M.U. Jones has noted of the Mucking excavation 'that direct evidence for the agriculture of the thousands of people who left their mark on the 40 acres behind Walton Hall farm during the two millennia from Neolithic to Saxon times is not nearly so easy to find, since most of the 2000 stone artifact fragments are from rotary querns (hand-turned millstones) and occasional saddle querns. But the discovery of actual grain during

the excavations was quite rare.' She points out that impressions of grain and straw were often used on pottery as decoration and that cylindrical pits on prehistoric sites usually interpreted as being cellars for storage were common in Mucking. This theory also accounts for one use for the ancient deneholes at Hangman's Wood, West Thurrock and elsewhere locally.

Among the earliest sites for engineering ingenuity in the new industries were the Purfleet quarries, and documents in the Essex Record Office give a glimpse into the expansion of lime and chalk quarrying here from the 1550s. In 1738 a lease of the quarry was purchased by a company which had been set up to supply 'Persons of the Trade and Mystery of Tilers and Bricklayers with all sorts of Goods necessary for the Said Trade'. From a simple enterprise winning chalk and lime from the prolific cliffs the business had grown by 1794, when the company sold out to Samuel Whitbread, into an impressively large and technical concern. Whitbread straight away introduced further improvements by constructing a railway at the cost of nearly £6,000, said to have been the first railway in Essex, and one that was particularly

94   Aveley Mill in May 1902. This post-mill looms above the miller, his wife and their daughter.

admired by Arthur Young when he surveyed the economy of Essex in 1807. Prior to Whitbread's ownership a way of working the chalk that used natural channels in the cliff to conduct the quarried chalk to the base had been found. This method explains the isolated blocks of chalk cliff that were prominent at the beginning of the 20th century, when after fifty years the quarries were opened again. Young describes the operation of the horse-drawn railway in 1807:

> One horse draws five or six wagons loaded … the railways lead to the bottom of the cliff to receive loam which is shovelled down to large wooden hoppers, which pour it at once into the carts, by means of the skeleton chalk rock being left in forms that conduct it. Ways lead hence also for delivering the broken chalk directly to the kilns, which for this purpose are built in a deeper excavation; and coals are distributed by other [rail]ways. From the kilns distinct iron roads lead also to shipping for delivery of the lime; the wagons are backed to the ship or barge side, and unloaded at once by tilting them up.

Much is revealed about the works in Whitbread's time by John Clarkson, who managed them and wrote letters to his employer. He mentions that their most important product was lime, and there were five limekilns on the site – a sixth kiln may have been built after 1812. The kilns were lighted most of the time, supplying a huge trade with London. Some of it went to the Drury Lane theatre, rebuilt after a fire, when Whitbread partly funded the cost. Much lime from Purfleet was sold to farms, and broken chalk was another product used by farmers on their land. Carts would come from ten to twenty miles away to carry away material from the quarry but there was also a considerable waterborne distribution, the works owning barges of its own among the many others plying the river. Other quarries were opened at Stifford, Grays and Little Thurrock where the chalk outcrop seemed to promise profit. The loam from the quarries at Purfleet was used as ballast for shipping for many years.

95 Whitbread's chalk quarry at Purfleet with the earliest railway in Essex. This print also shows how chalk is worked from the cliff and funnelled downwards in clefts made in the surface. It seems to have been a hazardous operation.

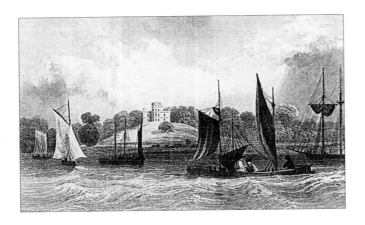

96 (*left*)   Fishing and other vessels in the
Thames in front of Belmont Castle, Grays in
the early 19th century.

97 (*below*)   Scottish smack boats pictured by
E.W. Cooke in the mid-19th century. They
unloaded cargoes locally and took on beer for
Scotland. These boats even provided a passenger
as well as a goods service.

Keith Bannister has recorded his memories of a Grays chalk pit in the 1920s. Entered through a narrow section next to the library, by the 1920s this pit was divided into three sections. The southern section near the library contained the ruins of an old lime-burning kiln and two or three small chalk hills that had become a children's playground. Going north, the centre of the pit contained Thomas Ward's 'Titan' works with much machinery and the giant block setting crane as a main feature. The northern section was still being worked for the extraction of chalk. Runnels were hand-cut by men suspended on ropes picking away at the face, with the loosened chalk rolling down the runnels into tip trucks put in place by horses. The full trucks were formed into trains which were taken away by a locomotive running through a tunnel under

Hogg Lane and finally crossing London Road towards Thomas Ward's quayside installation. The Globe Works (Charles Wall Ltd) stood on the site of a former brickworks between Rectory Road and Whitehall Lane at the beginning of the 20th century, on the borders of Grays and Little Thurrock. This site was typical of the complicated pattern in Thurrock's pit areas of successive enterprises making use of an industrial location. A huge excavation stretched back up Whitehall Lane to the deepest section behind Farley House, later the Urban District Council offices. Chalk was still being worked at the back of this quarry then removed to the Globe jetty and loaded onto Norwegian and Dutch boats. The former brickworks here had been owned for a time by a silver ore prospecting company. Shiploads of ore were brought from Australia

98 One of the innumerable railway locomotives serving the industrial railway lines and sidings in Thurrock. This one is seen on the tracks of the Purfleet Deep Water Wharf in the mid-20th century.

for crushing in order to extract the silver. The original brickworks reached as far as the old farm cottages in Rectory Road. Brick earth was won from the 'malm' pits in the Salisbury and Kent Road areas while the supply lasted. The bricks were then carried by rail under Whitehall Lane and Bridge Road and baked in kilns located on the south of the present Clarence Road. The railway then ran along where York Road is now to Landfield's wharf.

Among a number of important contracts carried out by the Globe Works was the construction of prefabricated iron sections for the new Vauxhall Bridge. These were taken to London on a steam traction engine which drew a couple of trailers, a man with a red flag

walking in front. The building department of Charles Wall was responsible for the *Felix Hotel* at Felixstowe in 1903. Teak, being the major part of the structure, was shipped from abroad, floated on rafts to the Globe jetty and then carried by the 'Jumbo' rail line under the Broadway and into the works. Another big contract was the Napsbury Asylum near St Albans, built from pitch pine. The works were also involved in laying the foundations of County Hall in London.

An unnamed brickworks in Grays was said to employ 500 men in making bricks for the construction of the Martello Towers along the east coast of Essex and Suffolk during the Napoleonic era in June 1808. East coast Martello Towers each needed 700,000 bricks for their completion. Daniel Defoe, the famous novelist, was at one time involved in a pantile factory at Tilbury of which he subsequently became the owner. He had hoped that tiles and bricks previously produced mainly in Holland would be the key to making his fortune, and plunged the whole of his stipend as Accountant to the Commissioners of the Glass Duty into this enterprise. Incredibly for such a rural undertaking, he employed one hundred families on the windswept marshes, making a profit of £600 a year. In 1697 he was supplying bricks for the new hospital at Greenwich. One wonders where his workers came from, bearing in mind the sparsely populated locality. Unfortunately Queen Anne's accession to the throne meant less tolerance for dissenters from the established church, of which Defoe was one. While spending time in prison in May 1703,

99 Receipt issued by brickworks at Little Thurrock in the mid-19th century showing the different types of brick made.

and before and after a warrant was put out for his arrest, the business was running at a loss. His tiles, although well made, were not being sold, the factory closed down and Defoe lost several thousand pounds. A biographer mentions a visit to Tilbury in 1860, when the excavations for the railway were being done, in the course of which the workmen unearthed tiles and bricks still in perfect condition. These aroused great interest among them when the link with the great writer was pointed out.

The 1848 directory entry for Meeson, Errington & Co. describes them not only as a coal, corn, lime, etc. merchant listed at Grays Wharf, but also as brick and tile makers. Another listing is for John Williams, also a brick and tile maker at Grays. The value of the Thames bank as a site for industry was that it enabled heavy goods to be carried off promptly by water transport. Dates for the prominent cement firms are given in Fig. 2 below. The Grays Gas Works (Grays Thurrock Gas and Coke Co. Ltd) began production in 1853. By 1884 it was a statutory undertaking and from then on operated as the Grays and Tilbury Gas Co. The company acquired four small undertakings in south-east Essex in 1913, enlarging their area of supply to places 10 to 15 miles away. The small works were closed and the Grays works was improved to produce the necessary capacity. They were north of the London, Tilbury and Southend railway line. A spur line which ran round to the north on the eastern side of the works served Grays chalk quarries, South Essex waterworks and brickworks. It then ran back past the gasworks and under the main line, providing a link with industries on the Thames bank, and there was a pier on the river with sidings. A gantry crane stood beside the gasworks siding and it is thought

100 The Dutch House in old Grays High Street shows the ingenuity and charm involved in building in local brick. Dutch foremen and workers were employed in obtaining chalk locally for embanking the sea walls on Canvey and at Dagenham when the river broke into these marshes.

1870	BROOKS SHOOBRIDGE & CO., Grays
1872	MESSRS GIBBS & CO. LTD, West Thurrock (in 1887 rotary kiln was first tried here)
1874	TUNNEL PORTLAND CEMENT, West Thurrock
1874	LION CEMENT WORKS (became the Wouldham Cement Works and later (1900) the Wouldham Cement Co. Ltd.)
1880	ROCK CEMENT CO., Rainham (later Rainham Cement Co. and New Rainham Cement Co. Ltd)
1900	ASSOCIATED PORTLAND CEMENT CO. formed (took over Messrs Hilton, Anderson, Brooks & Co. Ltd of Grays, Messrs Gibbs & Co. Ltd of West Thurrock and the New Rainham Portland Cement Co. Ltd)
1925	FONDU WORKS at West Thurrock erected (only makers of aluminous cement in British Isles).

Fig 2   Prominent cement firms in Grays Thurrock.

that coal was delivered and coke from the works was sent out this way, although roads were also used to service the works. Forty-five million cubic feet of gas produced in 1900 rose to 78 million by 1910. After 1913 production increased: 226 million cubic feet in 1922, 300 million in 1930. The Gas Light and Coke Co. took over in the latter year and production stopped on 4 December 1931. A remaining gas holder stands as a memorial of this enterprise and has been used for storage.

Seabrooke and Sons' Brewery began about 1800 in Grays High Street. In 1819 a new site was acquired at the southern end of Bridge Road. These new premises were surrounded by plenty of land for expansion purposes. Distribution by road and river was joined by the advent of the new railway line which ran right past the works. The brewery acquired the Congregational church adjoining, adding to its capacity, and there was also an extension by 1899 on the west side of Bridge Road. In 1929 the firm employed 180 hands and covered six and a half acres. Its own railway sidings joined it to the L.T.&S.R. line and also a Thames wharf. It owned about 120 public houses and, just as it was considering an increase in its trade, and had even started expanding its premises, there was a bolt from the blue: Messrs Charrington & Co. of Mile End made an offer that could not be refused, obviously intended to cut out competition, and closed the Grays brewery down within a couple of months, 140 men and 40 women being made redundant. It seemed that Charringtons had acquired a controlling interest which ensured the takeover would be successful.

101 (*left*)   A surviving gas holder north of London Road, Grays.

102 Seabrooke and Son's Brewery delivery cart on its rounds early in the 20th century.

103 A typical crate of four flagons of beer illustrated on the cover of Seabrooke's Price List.

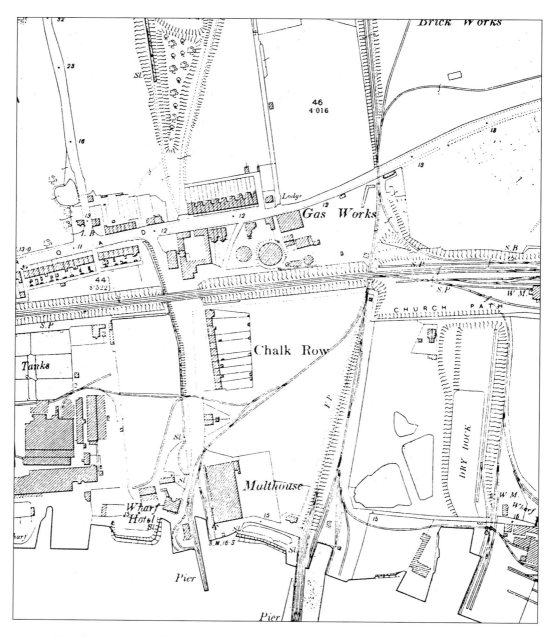

104 Map showing the Gas Works, north of the LTSR line in Grays, with other industrial installations in this small area in the early 20th century. The Thames wharves, piers and docks fill the bottom of this area.

105   Essex Board was produced by T.B.M. for lining ceilings and walls, as here in the Welfare Hall at Purfleet.

In 1951 there was a line of modern factory buildings along the north bank of the Thames from Hole Haven in the east to Purfleet in the west. These Thameside factories had flourished particularly from the later part of the 19th century and their agglomeration saw a process of acceleration in the twentieth. Oil refining and storage developed progressively from the 1930s, and by 1951 one of the largest crude oil distillation units in the UK was in operation. It was said at the time that, 'Employment is also provided for many thousands of people by the largest edible oil refiners and margarine manufacturers in the world, the largest concern of its kind in Europe making paper board, the largest exporter of rubber and leather footwear in the UK and the largest continuous soap factory in the country'.

The Shell refinery had been set up at Shell Haven (this name existing centuries before the Shell company arrived) in 1916. In fact, the first cargo of petrol was landed at Thames Haven in barrels in 1876; the successful local company London and Thameshaven Oil Co. Ltd began in 1898 on the same river frontage, later becoming known by the acronym LATHOL. The Vacuum Oil Co.'s Coryton refinery opened on 27 May 1984, taking over a site that had previously been Cory's and, prior to that, Kynoch's explosives factory. Vacuum oil later became the Mobil Oil Co. Van den Berghs and Jurgens Ltd Stork margarine works had originally been built in 1918 after the Dutch firm (at the beginning, two separate enterprises) were supposedly invited by the British government to start operations here. Thames Board Mills Ltd, a firm again founded

106 (*above*)   Some of the workforce and officers of Thames Board Mills at Purfleet greet a young and newly proclaimed Queen Elizabeth who is making a tour of inspection on 13 February 1953, on a visit to the Thameside areas that had been flooded.

107 (*left*)   Thames Board Mills' famous product 'Fiberite' caused a revolution, enabling boxmakers to produce a bright, attractive container for many household-name products.

108 A main factory building at Bata. The company eventually had a chain of 300 shops across Britain. At one time it held the record for footwear exports, sending 4,205,000 pairs overseas in 1952. Three thousand people were employed and the company even opened its own technical college in 1948.

by European owners, took over a small mill at Purfleet in 1902 which had changed names several times previously. In 1909 Fiberite cases were first made here. By 1966 T.B.M. produced around 45 per cent of the British output of paperboard for packaging, using salvaged waste paper as 85 per cent of its total raw material, the balance consisting of imported wood pulp.

One of the most surprising stories of Thurrock's industry concerns Thomas Bata, a Czech entrepreneur who acquired 650 acres of land on the East Tilbury marshland in 1932. His idea was to set up a factory to make footwear, and develop a model community self-sufficient in many ways. Hotels, housing, a garage, cinema and many other facilities were part of the scheme, which involved a certain amount of benevolent control of people's lives by the company. By 1933 the first single-storey building had been

erected and the experiment had met with a surprising amount of success, employees often being provided with modern housing close to the factory and shopping area in exchange for observing company discipline in working practices. During the Second World War the factory, like other parts of riverside Thurrock, was under the flight path of incoming German bombers but the community developed efficient air-raid precautions and its own Home Guard.

Hedleys commenced building a very modern works with large areas of glass in 1937. By May 1938 the superstructure was in place. Production of Fairy Soap began in late 1939, just as war had started, but full-scale production was in progress in 1940. Mention is also made in the 1951 booklet of the 30 members of the Thurrock Association of Industries. These give an idea of some of the other industries that made the Thurrock area the

109 An aerial view of British Bata's factory and housing, created from scratch in 1933. A Czech entrepreneur making rubber and leather footwear established a whole community on the bleak East Tilbury marshland acres.

hive of industry it was at this time. Apart from those already mentioned, they are: The Alpha Cement Co. Ltd; the Anglo–American Oil Co. Ltd; the Arcright Welding Co; the Beaconstone Co. Ltd; the British Carbo Norit Union Ltd; Messrs A. Bruce & Co.; Messrs Cole & Lecquire Ltd; Cory Bros & Co. Ltd; W.M. Cory & Son Ltd; Cubro & Scrutton Ltd; Drums Ltd; R. & H. Green and Silley Weir Ltd; Harrisons (London) Ltd; Magnet Timber Ltd; Purfleet Deep Wharf and Storage Ltd; Thurrock Chalk & Whiting Co. Ltd; the Thurrock Flint Co. Ltd, and William Thyne Ltd.

110 (*left*)   Advert dating from after the Second World War for the unique aluminous cement, completely immune to sulphate, sea water, sulphurous fumes and some weak acids. The Fondu Works, West Thurrock, originally erected in 1925 but later rebuilt, were the only manufacturers of this cement in the British Empire.

EIGHT

Only Connect: The Story of Transport

The river has always been an important means of getting to London and places in between, as well as those further away, and traders have travelled up the Thames from far away almost since there were products to trade with. Inland, the main road from Tilbury and Grays to the outside world ran north through Stifford and South Ockendon or via Aveley. Sandy Lane, going west from Mill Road, Aveley to Wennington, Rainham and London, was the west end of an old road from Wennington to Stifford which bypassed Aveley village. Romford Road in 1359 and after was known as Bredle Street and was thought, in the 18th century, to have been a Roman road. All these older roads relied on bridges to cross the frequent streams. An early

III The Tilbury-Gravesend ferry *Edith* ploughs its way across the Thames. This particular service linked the railways on either side of the Thames from about 1849. The steamboat of the same name was built in 1911 as a vehicle ferry but was altered to a passenger boat in 1927. She was replaced in 1961 by the diesels *Catherine* and, once again, *Edith*.

No. 1015.

GRAYS PIER COMPANY.

NOTICE IS HEREBY GIVEN, that Two of the London and Blackwall Railway Boats will, on and after Monday the 4th of April, and until further notice, call at the Grays Pier for Passengers for London, at the hours of EIGHT and HALF-PAST ELEVEN EVERY MORNING, Sundays included, AND EVERY AFTERNOON at HALF-PAST THREE; and the Boats which leave Blackwall, AT NINE O'CLOCK in the Morning, and AT THREE and HALF-PAST FIVE o'clock in the Afternoon, will call at the Pier at Grays to land Passengers.

The London and Blackwall Railway Trains run every Quarter of an Hour between London and Blackwall, from Fenchurch-street, on Week days, and from the Minories on Sundays.

FREDERICK FRANCIS, Secretary.
New Bond-street, London,
23d March, 1842.

112 (*left*)   Notice of inauguration of the London and Blackwall Railway's boat service, 1842. There had been many attempts to improve the embarkation at Grays for the London boats, which originally involved a mid-river transfer to the Gravesend to London monopoly boats.

113 (*below left*)   J. Creed's card shows the *Worlds End* pub as it looked in the earlier 19th century, an embarkation point for the ferry of that era.

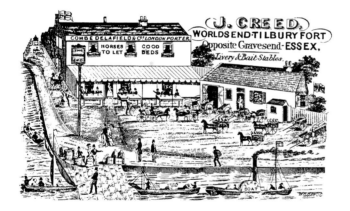

mention of Causeway (Cawsie) or Aveley Bridge over the Mardyke lying between Aveley and West Thurrock occurs in 1364. The bridge was believed to have been built by William Brinson in Edward II's reign. Later, a document of 1617 refers to Stifford Bridge, another important crossing of the Mardyke. Inhabitants of Stifford parish had complained about its lack of repair to the Quarter Sessions on 2 October 1616. The Justices of the Peace issued a certificate stating,

we now therefore certify that we have … taken view thereof and find it … in great decay, and necessary, with speed, to be repaired; but by whom it was first made, or by whom it ought now to be amended upon the best enquiry we could make we cannot with any certainty determine, it being all of stone, but thereby not subject to often reparation, and as it appeareth to be of great antiquity; but as far as we can by any likelihood conjecture, it seemeth to have been first made by a public purse, being a common road, both from Orsett and other parts there adjoining to London, and from Brentwood to divers ferries for passage into Kent … We have also made a survey by divers sufficient masons of the charge it will necessarily require for reparation and find both by their opinions and by our own judgment, upon conference with others, that it cannot in any sort be performed under the sum of thirty pounds.

Stifford was obviously a very important bridge indeed and this scenario was probably repeated in Thurrock, as elsewhere, down the centuries until roads were made the business firstly of private

114   The ferry boat *Rose* positions herself in the tideway by the landing stage at Tilbury. Built by A.W. Robertson and Co. of London in 1901, she was withdrawn and sold in 1961 after 60 years of service. The ancient ferry service was affected by the opening of the Dartford-Purfleet road tunnel, and closed in 1964, two boats, the *Tessa* and the *Mimie*, being sold off.

115   The splendid new landing stage and Tilbury Riverside Station, designed to improve access to the large liners and other ships increasingly using Tilbury in the 1920s and '30s.

116   A member of the railway staff stands proudly in front of the flower garden at Ockendon Station on the Grays-Upminster line of the London, Tilbury and Southend Railway at the beginning of the 20th century.

turnpike companies and, later, local authorities. Samuel Pepys is thought to have taken this road to Tilbury on occasion, although he generally found it more convenient to go by the river.

It has been said that, with its valuable mineral deposits of various kinds, the growth of Grays would have been much faster, had it not been hampered by a lack of really good communication up to the 19th century. The east-west road, later London Road, was in the 1700s merely a local link between West Tilbury, Grays, West

Thurrock and Purfleet, which all remained rather remote communities. As a defence for the capital Tilbury Fort certainly increased the importance of the route, and some improvements were made. Latterday communications were helped enormously by the construction of sections of the London to Southend arterial road in the 1920s. Key points in the transport network were the ports of Grays and Purfleet and the ferry point at Tilbury opposite Gravesend. There were regular services by boat between Grays and

117   The LTSR named their engines after places along the railway line and this is *Corringham*, in immaculate order. The Gravesend destination involved transfer to the ferry at Tilbury for the last lap over the Thames.

London from early times, mention of these being made in a document of 1637. Before 1841, when Grays Pier was constructed and steamers regularly called there, Gravesend river steamers could be hailed by boats sent out from the riverside.

A number of horse coaches began to serve Grays. In 1810 there was one plying between Romford and Tilbury Fort. In 1838 a coach between London and Horndon ran through Grays daily. The 1817 *Post Office London Directory* lists the *Bull Inn* at Aldgate and the *Blue Boar Cellar*, Aldgate as London pick-up and dropping–off points for Grays coaches. These left London at 4 p.m. daily. Another coach left the *Talbot* at Whitechapel on Mondays and Fridays at 9 a.m. A wagon for goods departed from the *Bull Inn*

118   Ockendon Station about 1900 with a porter and his grandchild. Although the platform is uneven, there are plenty of ornate gas lamps to light the way for passengers after dark.

119 Stanford-le-Hope Station with its two platform buildings, level crossing and signal box was adequately furnished to serve the original village in the late 19th and early 20th centuries.

120 An industrial railway scene at West Thurrock.

A company was formed, and an Act of Parliament obtained about nine years ago, for the establishment of a new shipping port called Thames Haven, on a creek in Essex near Corringham and Fobbing … For want of funds this projected out-port of the metropolis has not yet been formed, though some active measures for realising the grand project were taken in 1841; and no doubt it will ultimately be carried out. The design is to form a dock of 1,000 by nearly 900 feet, with 15 or 20 feet of water at spring tide ebbs; so as to be accessible to large vessels at all times of tide. The locality is considered highly favourable being the first sheltered part of the river, and where, from the action of the tide near Canvey Island,

at Aldgate on Monday, Wednesday and Friday at 8 in the morning. The directory notes a sailing vessel for Grays that left the Sheerness wharf, St Catherine's, London on Monday and Friday. White's *Directory* in 1848 states that

121 & 122 The tiny Corringham Railway, running from a terminus at Fobbing Road, Corringham and crossing the marshes to Coryton, was a unique line which was never part of the British Rail network. The top picture shows 0-6-0 locomotive number 2 on a train at Corringham platform. The picture below shows the other end of the line at Coryton, a 12-minute journey away. The line was originally built and opened for traffic in 1901 to serve the workers at the Kynoch explosives factory, bringing them to the works from Corringham and Fobbing. The name of the destination was originally Kynochtown and traffic was at its peak in the First World War when munitions production needed to be at the maximum. When Cory took over the facility the name changed to Coryton. These pictures show the line shortly before its closure in 1952.

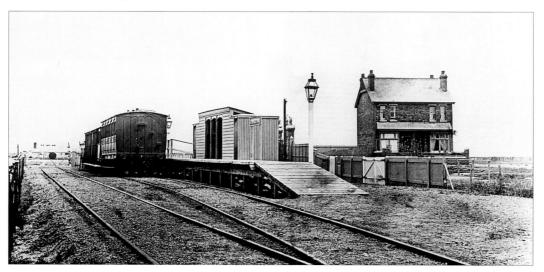

123 A full load of passengers on an early bus of Stanford and District services. The vehicle has boneshaker wheels and would have given a rough ride in the 1920s. One of its destinations was Grays and on the front and side of the vehicle are adverts for two shops in the town.

a deep water entrance is always secured. For the accommodation of steamers and their passengers, stone stairs are intended to be constructed, with warehouses for baggage and goods; and for the further acceleration of trade and intercourse with London, a railway is to connect the dock with the Eastern Counties Railway at Romford.

This two-fold project would

save 36 miles of river and crowded navigation, being an average of from 4 to 6 hours in time;

would bring Ostend, Calais, Boulogne, and Havre within a daylight certain voyage; would save the embarking and disembarking in small boats, and the delays of the London custom-house in clearing baggage, so that a traveller could get as far as Birmingham by Thames Haven, before he could clear at the custom-house, by going up the river. A railway has already been extended along the north side of the river, from the London Docks to North Woolwich, and has a branch to the Eastern Counties Railway at Stratford.

Of course, these schemes were not completed as envisaged, being overtaken when the London, Tilbury and Southend Railway was shortly afterwards approved and constructed. This opened in 1854 as far as Tilbury, with a station located at Grays, reaching Southend in 1856. The big port, when it came, was open in the form of Tilbury Docks and the later passenger landing stage; both had their own rail access from a loop line off the main route. Competition from the new Royal Albert Dock had forced the rival East and West India Dock Co. to decide upon a bold scheme for deep water docks 26 miles below London Bridge. The land needed was purchased and a Bill taken through Parliament in 1882. Although the dock was started in the same year it was April 1886 before the magnificent facilities were opened for business. The area of the dock was 56 acres which were entered from an open tidal basin of 18 acres. At first there was

124 (*top*) This single-decker bus serving route 374 between Grays and West Thurrock, Uplands Estate is waiting for its next trip alongside other London Transport vehicles, post-Second World War. An excellent network of services developed by the National Company served the Thurrock region before London Transport took over.

125 (*centre*) A somewhat later vehicle runs on the 370 from Grays, a route that still exists today. This was one of the vehicles absorbed from the previously independent bus companies when the London Passenger Transport Board was formed in 1933.

126 (*bottom*) Harris's Coaches have been a force in local transport for most of the 20th century, with a head office at 8 Parker Road, Grays. At one time in the 1950s they ran these 25-, 27- and 29-seater coaches.

some difficulty in securing trade, which led to a reduction in dock charges and a period of ruinous competition; the dock company had to make an arrangement with its rivals to work as one without any amalgamation of capital. Eventually the Port of London Authority was created to control all the docks and this led to stabilisation and gradual improvement, and extension to Tilbury during the 20th century. A phenomenon associated with the construction of the docks was the rapid development of the town of Tilbury, part of Chadwell parish, where no town had existed before.

NINE

On the Front Line

Very early in the history of Thurrock it was found necessary to construct defensive works on the lower reaches of the Thames. The Saxons who were once thought to be the opponents of the existing Romano-British inhabitants, may well, it is now thought, have constructed their string of settlements on the Thames banks in Thurrock and beyond to help the British defend the island from further invaders. Just beyond our borders to the east, Hadleigh Castle was erected in the 12th century on the downs which overlooked the entrance to the Thames. The castle originally had a courtyard 110 yards long. In 1371 a proclamation ordered that beacons and earthworks were to be built in the estuary to defend against raiders. At the time the French were causing havoc along the south coast of England and no doubt sometimes chanced their arm further afield.

In 1402 East Tilbury village was fortified by order of Henry IV, acquiring an earthwork. In 1539 Henry VIII gave the order to build blockhouses at East Tilbury and Tilbury Ness. The first monarch to be aware of the value of artillery, he set up a permanent force of gunners, appointing Hugh Boffield master gunner with four assistants, the idea being to create a system of cross-fire across the Thames with defenders on the Kent bank. The blockhouses were in the shape of a D, the rounded side facing the river. They consisted of two storeys and were built mainly of brick, absorbing 150,000 at a cost of £45 with stone dressings. It seems likely that the foundations were provided by chalk packing, 200 tons of chalk being bought at this time for this purpose. Captain Francis Grant was paid 12d per day in 1540 for being in charge of 'Johne's Bulwark'. The staffing also included a porter, two soldiers and four gunners, to be supplemented in emergencies by extra gunners and other personnel. In 1547 East Tilbury's blockhouse had its armament increased to 27 guns, having a maximum range of a mile. In the arbitrary way of decisions at the time, it was disarmed in 1553.

In 1558 the visit of Elizabeth I to the 'Camp Royal' at Tilbury included her famous speech to the assembled troops. The camp was sited on a sandy plateau close to West Tilbury church and must have been of considerable size as it is said in certain accounts that it reached as far as Biggin Heath two miles away. The show of

The Army of 1000 horse, and 22000 Foot, which ỹ Earle of Leicester comanded when hee Pitched his Tents att Tilbury

127 A playing card depicting the Armada camp at Tilbury in 1588, when it was visited by Elizabeth I.

strength was mounted at the time of the Armada crisis, when additional defence works of earth and timber had been swiftly constructed at both Tilbury and Gravesend to meet the possible threat of Spanish ships in the Thames. Other measures planned included a huge boom across the Thames made up of ships' masts, chains and cables attached to anchored lighters, and behind this a bridge of boats from Tilbury to Gravesend enabling troops to cross over into Kent should the Spanish forces land on the south coast. It was fortunate that the boom was not tested as it broke of its own weight. The Armada was

dispersed by a violent storm and the Thames forts were not needed.

West Farley church in Kent has a memorial to Edward, son and heir of John Lawrence, captain of the fort at East Tilbury in Essex who died on 8 April 1607. In the 17th century Tilbury Fort was enlarged and extended. The Board of Ordnance records state that parish constables of South Essex were to impress craftsmen and labourers to work on it. About a hundred craft workers in all were impressed, including nine from East Tilbury and eight from Grays.

In 1667 the Dutch fleet made an incursion up the Thames causing general alarm in London. Samuel Pepys writes on 24 July 1667:

> We got to Gravesend … and it grew darkish, and so I landed (and the flood being come) and went up to the *Ship* (Inn) and discoursed with the landlord of the house, who undeceives me in what I heard this morning about the Dutch having lost two men-of-war, for it is not so, but several of their fire ships. He do say, that this afternoon, they did force our ships to retreat but now they are gone down as far as Shield-Haven [Shellhaven].

Following these threats to the kingdom Sir Bernard de Gomme was called in to construct a massive new Tilbury Fort. At times nearly 300 men were impressed for the work, resulting in a very complex fortification, but it was ten years before the garrison was adequately armed, and even in 1680 Sir Bernard commented that a considerable amount of work remained to be done.

The early 1700s saw large powder magazines and improved barracks. Daniel Defoe thought 'they must be bold fellows who will venture in the biggest ships the world has heard of to pass such a battery'. In 1799 a renewed French threat saw four 24-pounder cannon placed in a battery

128 The attractive design on the main entrance of the Tilbury Fort belies its warlike intentions. This late 18th-century view shows a 'redcoat' soldier guarding the gate. Its mere existence, along with the other forts towards the mouth of the Thames, seems to have been enough of a deterrent; the fort's defences were never tested by enemy action nor a repeat of the Dutch Navy's incursion to this point in the 17th century.

129 Coalhouse Fort was built originally as a blockhouse to help defend the Thames and the access to London it provided.

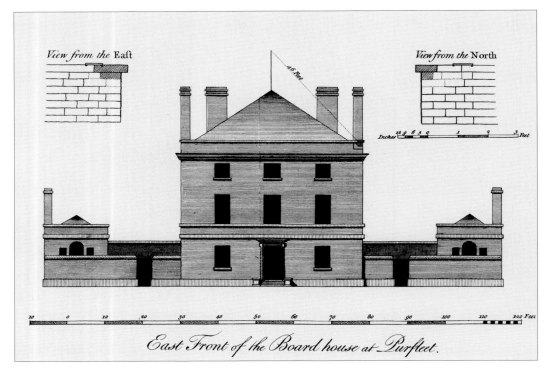

130 Engraving of the Ordnance Board house at the Purfleet Gunpowder Magazine, showing where the parapet was struck by lightning. Lightning striking a more vital part of this installation would have obliterated the whole of Purfleet.

at East Tilbury approximately where the present open battery at Coalhouse Fort is located, and the general rearmament of the Tilbury forts as well as those lower down the Thames. After the French were defeated at Waterloo another disarmament took place at the local forts. In 1861 a new powerful Coalhouse Fort was designed to work in conjunction with ones at Shornemead and Cliffe to provide a first line of defence on the river. Many strengthenings of the Thames forts took place from this time to keep up with advancing military science. One notable figure supervising these changes was Colonel, later General, Charles Gordon in 1865. Today Thurrock is fortunate that both forts remain and

it is possible to learn more about their history.

At the other end of Thurrock, at Purfleet, a different kind of structure intimately associated with the defence of Britain was the Garrison and Royal Gunpowder Magazine which supplied land and sea forces from 1759, when it was moved here from Woolwich. A housing estate now occupies some of the site but the Clock Tower gateway and part of the former wall that surrounded the magazines is still intact, as is the last surviving powder magazine, number 5, and the Barrel Store (Copper Hoop Store) also once used as a chapel. Inside Magazine Number 5 there is now a comprehensive museum highlighting the history of the site and Thurrock's association with war and defence. The story of the removal of the gunpowder magazines to Purfleet is told in R.P. Cruden's *History of the town of Gravesend*:

> Several noblemen, gentlemen and others, inhabitants of Greenwich and places adjacent, represented to Parliament, that there was within a quarter of a mile of the town, a magazine, containing great quantities of gunpowder, frequently to the amount of 6,000 barrels; that, besides the great danger which must attend all places of that kind, the magazine stood in an open field, unclosed by any fortification or defence, consequently opposed to treachery and every other accident; alleging that, if this magazine should take fire, not only the lives and property of the petitioners, but also the shipping in the river would be destroyed. It was stated also, that the magazine was then in a dangerous condition, being supported on all sides by props that were decayed at the foundation; whereupon they prayed that the magazine might be removed to some more convenient place where an accident would not be attended with such dismal consequences … an Act was passed for purchasing ground at Purfleet, and for erecting there a magazine for gunpowder, for the land and sea-service, with barracks, guard-house, and other houses and buildings, necessary for the care and management of such magazines; and fifteen thousand pounds were granted for the purpose.

Obviously the influence wielded by the gentlemen of Greenwich and Woolwich far outweighed any consideration that might be given to the pleas of the humble cottagers of Purfleet who were to suffer the hazards and dangers of fire and explosion for the next 200 years.

Divine Providence somehow protected them. It seems incredible now that no serious incident occurred, although there were a few near-misses. In 1777, for instance, there was a lightning strike on one of the magazine buildings.

131 (*top*)   The gateway at the Purfleet Gunpowder Magazine, and part of a curtain wall which at one time completely surrounded the premises. A strong garrison of troops guarded the magazines.

132 (*above*)   A view of Purfleet in 1807. The magazines were to the left of the prominent *Royal Hotel* building seen on this print. The gunpowder was often brought here via a pier and taken away in designated boats.

133 (*left*)   Two years before the outbreak of the First World War, on 12 June 1912 HMS *Thunderer* passes Purfleet.

134 (*below left*)   A network of rails assisted movement of heavy equipment within Coalhouse Fort. Extra installations were added to the fort in the Second World War.

In 1864 *Chamber's Journal* had this to say about the situation,

> It may be a question whether the Government is wise in concentrating the great reserve of powder in one magazine, and that in a position not inaccessible to an active enemy. It is doubtless very convenient, from its proximity to the principal powder-mills of the country and its facilities for shipment, but it would surely be wise to look upon it merely as a place for the receipt and inspection of, and not as the great depository of, our 'villainous salt-petre'.

Although the magazine buildings were enclosed by a wall and guarded by their own Soldiers, at times there seems to have been a rather relaxed attitude at the facility. For instance, in 1880 the building later known as the Magazine Fire Engine House was used as a public market for the weekly sale of provisions brought in from the neighbouring towns and villages. At times of crisis, such as the Crimean War, there were sometimes even more stores of gunpowder about Purfleet. During the period *c.* 1868–70, two hulks acting as floating magazines, the *Conquestador* and *Mermaid*, were moored in the Thames at 'Aveley Hole' just above Purfleet Creek, and were full of surplus gunpowder because the Purfleet magazine itself was congested. Previously these two vessels had been moored even closer.

135 The Royal Engineers camp at Purfleet with a soldier reading the notices. Purfleet was used to soldiers guarding the gunpowder magazine, but in the First World War the village was full, with more soldiers in training or waiting to go to France. Soldiers also manned an anti-aircraft gunsite.

Due to the area's strong association with the Merchant Navy, many local people were lost at Sea in the First World War. The war also saw the first German aerial incursions which used the Thames to point the way to London, their target. This route was pioneered by the Zeppelins and similar military airships and later exploited by the Gotha bombers. A number of batteries of anti-aircraft gunners were ranged on either side of the Thames, including Thurrock, and on one memorable occasion concerted efforts by all

of them brought down a Zeppelin (LZ15). The detachment of Royal Garrison Artillery Gunners were credited among others with disabling the airship and forcing it to finally crash into the Thames. The Lord Mayor of London, grateful that an attack on the capital had been averted, was allowed by the War Department to present no fewer than 353 medallions to all the men involved and to the 42 gunners and two electrical engineers who had done such sterling work at the Purfleet Battery. During the war a large

contd on p.123

136   Among this hospital group of wounded soldiers is Private F. Reeve of 33 Salisbury Road. A soldier in the Bedfordshire Regiment, he later died of his wounds, his death being recorded in the *Grays and Thurrock Gazette* of 30 November 1918.

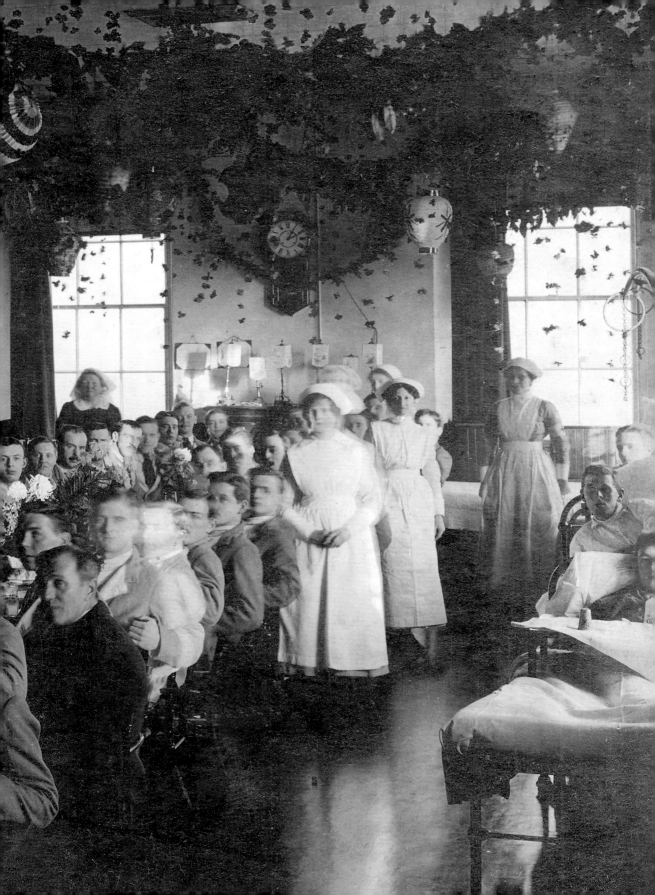

137 (*top left*)   Not, as often supposed, a Zeppelin over Grays in the First World War, but a later version attending an air display in the 1930s. Those who had suffered in that war might have looked fearfully upwards at this show of air power. The photograph, taken by R. W. Pigney over Lenthall Avenue, is jokingly inscribed: 'Colin Tyler's overalls and Graf Zeppelin – both airborne!'

138 (*centre*)   A Second World War flying bomb on display at Purfleet Magazine. These pilotless 'doodlebugs' frequently soared over the district before their engines, which sounded like a motorbike, cut out and they crashed to the earth. Unlike the later V2 terror weapon which allowed no time for reaction, falling from an invisible height at incredible speeds out of the blue, the progress of flying bombs could be traced against the sky and avoiding action taken when the red exhaust and noise stopped and a trajectory had been estimated.

139 (*bottom left*)   The badge of the 6th Anti-Aircraft Division, worn on the arm of the uniform, consisted of a black and white target with a red arrow piercing the bull. Their operational area covered the Thames estuary, Essex and North Kent.

140 (*opposite*)   This rhyming advert in the *Grays and Thurrock Gazette* exhorted the ordinary citizen to buy National Savings Stamps.

number of soldiers were billeted at every possible location in Thurrock, including schools and, of course, the barracks at Purfleet which had been used to accommodating soldiers. Many of the soldiers were trained locally before being sent to France.

The defensive batteries and other arrangements of the First World War were to be repeated along the Thames in the Second. On this occasion the fighting in France largely ceased with the Dunkirk evacuation, and the might of enemy air power meant even more emphasis was placed on air defence. But this war involved almost the whole civilian population, factories in the area being turned over to war production, for which many of them were ideally suited. Each factory had to consider how to evacuate its staff during aerial attack and adopt the national scheme of Air Raid Precautions (abbreviated to ARP). Factory staff often spent large parts of the day confined to their air-raid shelters, but these wartime factories played a large part in raising production.

As the *Essex and Thurrock Gazette* reported on 17 February 1945, Thurrock also played a significant part in the return of our troops to mainland Europe:

> The Thurrock area has played a prominent part in this war, and the people have been in the thick of it almost since the very commencement. But no event has thrilled the public more than the invasion of Normandy and the preparations leading up to it – the embarkation of troops, the shipment of supplies and of armaments, with Tilbury the centre of activities … Months before D-Day there was more than usual activity at the Docks. Hundreds of men were drafted into the district on works of great importance, the nature of which has not yet been fully disclosed … So far as the general public were concerned Tilbury was a closed book and anything connected with the Docks was referred to in whispers – a wink

141 (*right*) Soldiers stream over the footbridge at Purfleet, crossing the railway lines en route for the rifle ranges on the marshes.

142 (*below*) Radar or listening tower near the AA site beside the Thames at East Tilbury.

or a nod conveyed much in those days … All this time there had been a big concentration of troops and material over a wide area in Thurrock. Almost every plot of vacant ground was taken over by military vehicles. Big encampments sprung up overnight, and field kitchens and other necessary accommodation were built to cater for the troops in the vicinity. Many of the men never left their vehicles and slept in them at night-time. During their short stay in the district, the troops were made welcome and little luxuries were showered on them by a generous public. How this hospitality was appreciated has

been revealed by letters from men in France. Then suddenly there was renewed activity and the convoys rumbled on towards the Docks. Men and machines in continuous streams took possession of the highways which had been especially mapped out by indicators. All civilian traffic was brought to a standstill while at intervals the convoys passed. But even at this stage it was a mere trickle compared with what was to follow … At many places where the long lines of vehicles slowed down and stopped, the troops emptied their pockets, showering coins to excited youngsters on the pavements. Cups of tea and cakes were brought out by residents along the route. Tilbury especially was the scene of many such acts of hospitality. Two or three days before the announcement was made that a landing had been effected on the other side, military traffic increased considerably. Several of the men had their faces blackened, officers were unshaven and a more serious tone was reflected in the troops. Some were singing ditties popular in the last war, but the majority, with eyes fixed ahead, were silent and gave no indication of their true feelings. Almost every vehicle had its own particular slogan, and many would have made

143   Wartime anti-aircraft emplacement on the Thames bank in front of Coalhouse Fort at East Tilbury.

even Hitler and his gang blush. Most people thought the life of the ordinary civilian would be altered by demands of the military on road and rail transport, and that there would be other inconveniences, which everyone was quite prepared to put up with. But it did not turn out that way. So well had arrangements been made that the troops carried on as if an invasion was an everyday job.

TEN

Thurrock Since 1945

∽ひSℰଦ୨

Thurrock's population emerged from the Second World War anticipating a brave new world of opportunities for all. The industrial strip along the Thames had been concerned with the production of weapons and artefacts associated with the war effort. The difficulty of changing back to a peacetime economy was coupled with the enormous task of repairing the damage to local factories, houses and utilities caused by German bombers en route to London. The late 1940s and early 1950s saw a decade of hardship when continued rationing and 'make do and mend' resulted in a very basic standard of living for many. The national economy was depressed, a typical feature of postwar conditions. An escape route from the humdrum and rather spartan lifestyle was the twice-weekly visit to the cinema, where Americans could be seen enjoying the benefits of refrigerators, washing machines, modern kitchens and all the other accompaniments of the American Dream. Most people had yet to see the appearance of such luxuries at home. The Festival of Britain in 1951 aired many new ideas and designs, and the need to restart peacetime production of goods, at first to earn money from exports, opened

the door gradually to the new consumerism of the 1960s.

Before the war the project for a tunnel under the Thames between Dartford and West Thurrock/Purfleet had been started, and considerable progress had been made. This was halted when war broke and the restart was delayed by shortages of labour and materials. These vital resources were being diverted to provide essential repairs to Britain's damaged infrastructure. Scarce resources were needed to provide modern homes, of which there was a shortfall. Many homes had been destroyed during the war and many more were old and lacked basic facilities.

The London County Council had been making plans before the end of the conflict to decant a large part of the population out of damaged and overcrowded conditions in inner London. A ring of new estates and communities were to be created on open sites around the capital. The Aveley Estate was to be one of the largest, with a planned 5,200 dwellings. It would be sited on the parks and fields of the old Belhus country mansion and was soon to become known by this name. The development also needed schools, churches, libraries, clinics, community centres, open spaces, shops and also a considerable acreage for industry. Other suggested facilities, such as a cinema, did not materialise, and the new inhabitants had to travel to Grays, which was well provided with the State, the Regal and the Ritz. The Regal soon became a bowling alley, a popular new activity showing the influence of American ideas for the first time.

Few owned cars at this time, and bus services were provided between Belhus and other local centres, the only railway station being on the northern edge of the estate at Ockendon, on the Upminster-Grays branch. There was already a bus route between Romford and Grays (the 370 service). Rail communications were improved on the Tilbury, Grays and London Fenchurch Street line by the electrification in the 1960s of the previously steam-hauled services. Traditional council housing stock was increased in Tilbury and Chadwell St Mary, for example, the closure of many of the old extractive industries making available new sites for development. At first the smaller ones were taken over by utility companies and small engineering and similar firms.

When the Dartford-Purfleet tunnel eventually opened at the beginning of the 1960s, the Thurrock area was ready to be plugged into the emerging national motorway network. A second tunnel was opened in 1980, and the M25 arrived in Thurrock in 1984. The large

increase in local traffic caused by the road improvements created further pressures. Various widenings and improvements were made to the tunnel approaches and the toll-booth collection system, and what is now known as the Dartford Crossing was completed by the construction of the impressive Queen Elizabeth II Bridge, opened in 1991. Thurrock was now linked to the European road network via the Channel Tunnel. Plans to transform the centre of Grays faltered when a vast pit in West Thurrock was transformed to become the giant Lakeside Shopping Centre.

These factors have stimulated building in many of the Thameside areas vacated by the old industries and the cement works. There have been developments at Tilbury and along the Grays riverside frontage, but most importantly westward from Hogg Lane, just outside Grays town centre to the north. Here the massive Chafford Hundred scheme has laid housing over the old rubbish dump and Second World War anti-aircraft site, then over the worked-out quarries, to the borders of the railway line by the Lakeside Shopping Centre where a new Chafford Hundred station has been built. This has finally sparked a revival in Grays town, where a large supermarket has created a new focus to the western end of Grays, including a rebuilding of the bus station, provision of car parks and re-orientation of the road system.

Bibliography

❦

The Ambulator (11th edition 1811)

Barnes, B., *Grays Thurrock; a pictorial history* (1988)

Barnes, B., *Grays Thurrock revisited* (1991)

Carney, T.J., *Thurrock in the Twenties* (1990)

Evans, B., *Around Grays* (1994)

Evans, B., *Century of Thurrock* (1999)

Evans, B., *Thurrock past and present* (2002)

Morgan, G.H., *Forgotten Thameside* (1951)

Palin, W., *Stifford and its neighbourhood, past and present* (1871)

Palin, W., *More about Stifford and its neighbourhood* (1872)

Panorama (Journal of the Thurrock Historical Society) Nos 1 (1956) – 40 (Dec 2000)

Reynolds, R., *Thurrock; the Great War* (1998)

Reynolds, R. and Catton, J., *Thurrock goes to war (WW2)* (1997)

Sparkes, I.G. (comp.), *Bibliography of Thurrock* (1962)

Victoria County History of Essex, volume 8 (1983)

White, W., *History, gazetteer and directory of Essex* (1848)

Index

CRSD

Page numbers printed in **bold** type refer to illustrations

Agriculture, 15

Air Raid Precautions (ARP), 123

Ambulator, 19

Annandale (Steamship), **42**

Anti-Aircraft Defence, 119, **122**, **124**, **126**

Armada, 114, **114**

Associated Portland Cement, 96

Aveley, 87-88; Archaeology, 3, **4**, 7, 11; Bridge, 104; High Street, **84**, **85**; Lodge, **85**; Medieval times, 10; Mill, **90**; Pit, 3

Avenue North Building, **80**

Baker Street, 29; archaeology, 9

Balstonia, **48**, 53

Bampton, Thomas, 17

Barrel Store, 116

Bata, **100**, 101, **101**, **102**

Baud family, 54

Beaker People, 4

Belgic People, 7

Belhus, **87**, 88, **88**; archaeology, 9

Belmont Castle, 20, 23, 25, 26, **92**

Biggin Heath, 113

Bingley, Randal, 13

Bishop Bonner's Palace, **27**

Bishop Cedda's Palace, 11

Boffield, Hugh, 113

Bredle Street, 103

Brickworks, 93, 94, **94**, 95

Bridge of boats, 114

Bridge Road, **35**

Brinson, William, 104

Bronze Age, 5, **5**, 8; Axe, **5**

Brooks Shoobridge & Co., 96

Bruyns Manor, 61

Bull Inn, Corringham, **52**

Bulphan, 66, 67, **67**, 69; Church, **67**; Fen, 66, 67, 69

Buses, 110, **111**, 112, **112**

Button, Zachariah, 20, 23

Cade, Jack, 60

Calais (Staple of), 16

Campe Royall, 17, 113

Catton, Will, 16

Causeway Bridge, 104

Celtic Peoples, 8

Cely family, 16

Chadwell St Mary: 19th-century, 46, **46**, 48; archaeology, 8,9; Local Government, 33

Chalk and Whiting industry, 26, 89, 91

Churches (Noncomformist), 20

Ciment Fondu, 96, **102**

Clactonian Flint industry, 4

Coaches, **112**

Coal Road, **1**, **2**

Coal Trade, 57

Coalhouse Fort, 56, **115**, 116, **118**, **126**

Coastguard, 19

Cockley's Refreshments, 30

Coggers, 54

Cole, Henry, 17

Condovers, 17

Cornwall (Training Ship), **83**

Corringham, 17, **52**, 53, 54; archaeology, **5**; Marsh, 13;
    Railway, 109, **109**
Cory's, 99
Coryton, **109**
Cox and Palmer's Tea Garden, **81**
Cross Keys Inn, 48

D-Day preparations, 123-6
Danelaw, 12
de Bruyn family, 61
Defoe, Daniel, 94, 114
Deneholes, 6, **6**, 7, **7**
Domesday Record, 12
Doodlebugs, **122**
Drover, **56**
Dry Street, **68**
Dutch Coins, 17
Dutch Fleet in Thames, 18, 60, 114
Dutch House, **95**

East India Company, 40
East Tilbury, 55, **55**, 56, 113; archaeology, 5; Blockhouse, 133
Edith (Ferries), **103**
Elephant (Ancient), 3
Elizabeth I, 113
Elizabeth II, **100**
Empire Theatre, Grays, **25**
Essex Board, 99
Ewell, John, 17
Explosives manufacture, 99

Farming, 15, 89
Fen Lane, Bulphan, **70**
Fiberite, **100**, 101
Fishermen, 17
Fishing vessels, **92**
Fletthall, 73
Flooding, 83, 84
Fobbing, 17; Church, **58**; Marsh, 13
Footwear manufacture, **100**, 101, **102**
Ford Place, 71

Gas Light and Coke Co., **92**
Gasworks, London Road, 95, 96, **96**, **98**
Gibbs and Co., 96
Globe Works, 93

Godwin of Thurrock, 14
Goliath (Training Ship), **128**
Gomme, Bernard de, 114
Grant, Francis, 113
Grantham family, 82, 83
Gray, Henry de and family, 14, **14**, 20
Grays: archaeology, 4, 5, 7; Brewery, 19; Chalk Pit, 93;
    Church, 134, 14, **19**, 20; Coastguard, 19; Co-operative
    Society Wharf, 38; Football Club, **24**; Gasworks, 95,
    96, **96**, **98**; High Street, 2, **20**, **25**; Lime Quarries, 19;
    Local Board of Health, 33; London Boat, 108; London
    Coaches, 107; Market Charter, 18; Market House, 19;
    Medieval Grays, 18; Old High Street, **26**, **95**; Orsett
    Road, 11; Pier, 19; Pier Company, **98**; Port, 18, 19, 106,
    107; Post Office, 21; Workhouse, 33
Grays Market, 25; 19th-century, 19, 20; 20th-century, **20**
Grays Thurrock United F.C., **24**
Grices, 64, 66
Groves Manor, 61
Gunpowder Magazines, 110, 114, **116**, **117**, 118

Hangman's Wood, 28; Deneholes, **7**; Path, **1**, **2**
Harris Coaches, **112**
Headley's, 101
Henry VIII, 113
Hewers, Thomas, 21
Hilliard, George R., 20
Holdstocke, William, 28
Homesteads Ltd, **48**
Horncastles Stores, **27**
Horndon London Coach, 107
Horndon-on-the-Hill, 17, 64; Church, 66, **66**; South Hill,
    65; Wool Market, 16
Hotoft Charity, 31

Ice Age, 3
Industrial Railways, **93**, 95, **108**
Iron Age, 5, 6, 7, 12

Jackson, Martha, 48
Joyes Department Store, 25, 26

Kempster, William, 36
Knevynton, Ralph de, 15, **15**
Knights Hospitaller of St John, 14
Kynoch's Explosives Factory, 99, 109

Langdon Hills, 17, 69, 70
Lanham and Pennington Ltd, **22**
Larkins, Orsett, 15
Lawrence, John, 114
Linford archaeology, 6, 7, 11
Lion Cement Works, 96
Listening Tower, **124**
Little Thurrock, **4**, **43**, 43-6, 91
Little Thurrock Brickworks, 93, **94**
London Boat: Blackwall Railway, 104; Gravesend Vessel,
    19, 106-7, **104**
London Tilbury and Southend Railway, 86, 111, **107**

Mammoth, 3
Manor of Thurrock (Grant), 14, **14**
Manorial Accounts, 15
Mardyke River, 67, 69, 71,73, 104
Marshes, 13
Martello Towers (bricks for), 94
Medieval era, 12, 13
Meeson, Errington and Co., 95
Mill Lane Pit, 6
Mobil Oil Co., 99
Mucking, 54, 55
Mucking Excavation, 4, 8, 9, **9**, 10, **10**, 11, 12, 13
Mucking Marsh, 54

New Jenkins, 54
New Road shops, **24**, **29**, **35**
Norman era, 12
Norman farming, 12
North Road, South Ockendon, **65**
North Stifford, 71, **72**, 73
Norwegian Seamen's Mission, **41**

Ockendon Station, **106**, **107**
Ockendon Stores, 68
Oil refining and storage, 99
Old Hall Farm, Orsett, **27**
Old Hall Manor, 54
Ordnance Board House, Purfleet, 116
Orsett, 1, 27, 28; in 1848, 29; archaeology, 6, 7, 9; Charity
    School, 31, 32; Church Tower, 28; Manor, 27; Post
    Office, **32**; Rural District, 32, 33, 34; Rural Sanitary
    Authority, 33; Thatchers, 28; Union Workhouse, 31, 32,
    33; Village, **32**

Palaeolithic tools, **4**
Palin, William, 71
Palmer's School, 20, 21, **22**, 23; original building, **19**
Peasants' Revolt, 59
Pepys, Samuel (diary entries), 18, 114
Pilgrims, 75, 78, 79
Place-names, 11, 13
Pleistocene era, 3
Pliny the Elder, 13
Police, 36
Poll Tax Riot (1381), 17
Porter, Thomas, 16
Purfleet, 74, **76**, **78**, 79, 80, **80**, **81**, 82-4, 86-7, **99**, **116**, **117**,
    118, **118**, **119**, **124**; Chalk Works, 82, 83; Deep Water
    Wharf, **93**; Inns, 82; Level Crossing, 82; Powder Magazine,
    116, **116**, 117, **117**, 118, **122**; Quarries, 89; Railway, 86
Purfleet Road, Aveley, **86**
Purveyance (Royal Custom), 18

Quoits, 34

Railway Terrace, **81**
Railways, 86, **106**, **107**, **109**, 110, 111
Recreation Ground (Grays), **24**, **30**
Rectory Road (Little Thurrock), **43**
Reeve, Private F., **120**
Rich family, 17
Roads, 103-8
Rock Cement Co., 96
Romano-British culture, 9, 10, 13
Romano-British pottery, 7
Romans, 7, 8, 9, 13; farming, 10; food, 10-11; pottery, 10;
    roads, 103; villas, 10; wells, 10
Rose (Tilbury Ferry), **105**
Royal Engineers' Camp, Purfleet, **119**
Royal Hotel, **117**
Royal supplies, 18
Rugward, 13
Russian cargo vessels, 42

St Chad, 57
St Clere's Hall, 54
St Mary Magdalene Church, 57
Salmon's Travelling Shop, **28**
Saltmaking, 13
Saltonstall family, 61

Sandy Lane, 103

Savings Stamps, **123**

Saxons, **9**, 11, 54, 113; bucket, **9**; glass horn, **17**; 'Hall', 12; place-names, 11

Saxton's shop, **20**

Sea Wall, 56; collapse, 83

Seabrooke and Sons Brewery, 96, **97**

Shaa family, 17, 66

Sheep: bells, **16**, 17; fair (sheep and cattle), 16; pasture, 16; for Royal Court, 18

Shell Refinery, 99

Ship Inn, Little Thurrock, **44**

Shipman shops, 36

Slade's Hold, 31

Slatey House, 13

Sleepers Farmhouse, **46**

Smack Boats, **92**

Smallpox, 32, 34

Smugglers, **58**, 59

Socketts Heath, 29

South Ockendon, 61-4, **61**, **62**, **64**, **65**; Hall, 62-3, **62**; Methodist Church, 64

South Stifford, 71, 73

Southend Road, 29, **34**

Stanford and District (Bus) Service, **110**

Stanford-le-Hope, 17, **41**, 48-9, 53, **48**, **49**, **50**; archaeology, 7; Railway Station, **108**; sheep pasture, 16

Stifford Bridge, 71, 104

Stifford Hall, 71

Stifford Heath, 71

Stifford Parish, 104

Straw, Jack, 17

Swanscombe Man, 3

Terp Mounds, 13

Thames Board Mills, 99, **99**, **100**, 101

Thames: Defences, 113-16, **114**, **115**, 123; Haven, 60, 99, 108, 110; River, 37-42, 103, **103**

Thames traffic: 19th-century, 19, 104; medieval, 18

Theobald, James, 20

Thoroughgood, Ralph, 54

Thunderer (HMS), **118**

Thurrock Association of Industries, 101

Thurrock Manor (Grant), 14

Thurrock Museum, 17

Thurrock Urban District Map (1936), **2**

Thurrock Urban District Offices, 93

Tilbury, 2, 94, 125; and D-Day, 125; Archaeology, 11; Armada Camp, 17; Docks, 39-40, **39**, **40**, 42, 111, 112; Ferry, 56, 103, **103**, **105**; Fort, **57**, 106, 114, **115**; Hailing Station, **40**; Landing Stage, **105**; Man, 4; Marsh, 16, 17; Passenger Port, 41-2; Port, 32-3; Riverside Station, 42; Seamen's Hospital, **41**; Tilbury Fort-Romford coach, 107; Urban District, 33-4

Tilemakers, 95

Tileworks (Defoe's), 94

Tillaburgh, 57

Titan Works, 93

Turold of Rochester, 13, **13**

Typhoid, 33

Vacuum Oil Co., 99

Van den Berghs and Jurgens Ltd, 99

Vandenanker, Cornelius, 83, 84

Wade Wyke, 13

Ward, Thomas, 93

Watt family, 89

Webb, Richard, 20, 25

West Lee Chapel, 57

West Thurrock, 73, 74, 75; archaeology, 8; council homes, 34; Manor, 84; Schools, **74**; shop (Teece's), **75**

West Tilbury, 56, 57, 59, 113; Church, 57; Marshes, 17

Westelward, 13

Whitbread family, 80, 83, 84, 86, 89

Whitbread's Chalk Quarry, **91**

White Lion, Fobbing, **59**

Whitehall Lane Pit, 3, 46, 93

Whitehall Road, 23

Whitmore family, 28, 29

Williams, John, 95

Wilson, Matthew, 23

Wool Market (Horndon), 16

World War One, 119, **119**, **120**, 123

World War Two, 123-6, **124**, **126**

World's End pub, 104, **104**

Young, Arthur, **91**

Zeppelins, 119, **122**

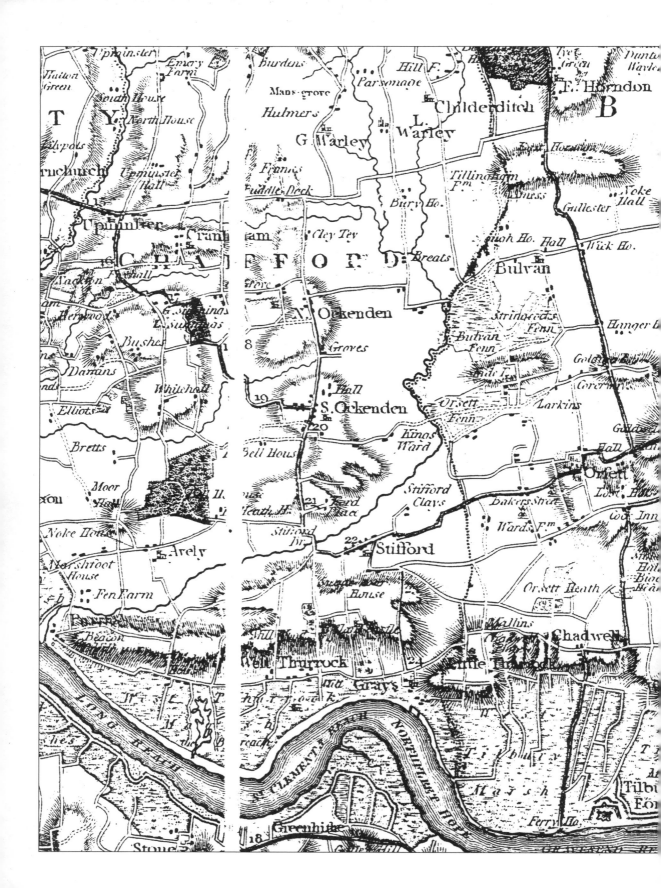